David Spencer

Early Baptists of Philadelphia

David Spencer

Early Baptists of Philadelphia

ISBN/EAN: 9783337008369

Printed in Europe, USA, Canada, Australia, Japan

Cover: Foto ©Lupo / pixelio.de

More available books at **www.hansebooks.com**

THE
EARLY BAPTISTS

OF

PHILADELPHIA.

BY

REV. DAVID SPENCER.

PHILADELPHIA:
WIILLIAM SYCKELMOORE
1877.

Entered according to Act of Congress, in the year 1877, in the Office of the Librarian of Congress at Washington, D. C.

PHILADELPHIA:
WILLIAM SYCKELMOORE, PRINTER,
No. 1420 Chestnut Street.

TO THE MEMORY OF

REV. SAMUEL JONES, D. D.,

WHO, FROM HIS GRADUATION AT THE UNIVERSITY OF PENNSYLVANIA,
MAY 18TH, 1762, TO HIS DEATH AT LOWER DUBLIN, FEBRUARY 7TH, 1814,
WAS A NOBLE REPRESENTATIVE OF THE EARLY BAPTISTS OF PHIL-
ADELPHIA; FOREMOST IN THE AGGRESSIVE WORK OF OUR DE-
NOMINATION; GENEROUS IN HIS SYMPATHIES WITH ALL
WHO LOVED THE LORD JESUS; BENEFICENT IN HIS EF-
FORTS TO ADVANCE MENTAL AS WELL AS SPIRITUAL
CULTURE; PATRIOTIC IN HIS DEVOTION TO THE
INTERESTS OF HIS COUNTRY; THE FRIEND
OF THE NEEDY; HOSPITABLE AND COUR-
TEOUS TO ALL; THIS WORK IS MOST
RESPECTFULLY DEDICATED

BY THE AUTHOR.

ILLUSTRATIONS.

Rev. Samuel Jones, D. D.	*Frontispiece*
Barbadoes Storehouse.	32
Christ, Protestant Episcopal, Church.	38
Montgomery Baptist Meeting House.	52
Southampton Baptist Meeting House.	70
Hopewell Academy.	76
Lagrange Place Meeting House.	87
Carpenter's Hall.	108
Independence Hall.	119
Old Meeting House at Roxborough.	147
Lower Dublin Baptist Meeting House.	163
First Church Broad and Arch Streets.	194

CONTENTS.

CHAPTER I.—1684—1690.—Philadelphia Founded.—Religious Liberty.—Welsh Parentage.—Origin of Baptists.—John Holme Purchases Land.—Rev. Thomas Dungan.—Cold Spring Church.—Bucks and Philadelphia Counties.—William Penn and Thomas Dungan.—An English Baptist.—A Celebrated Spring.—Persecution in Wales.—Settlement at Pennypack.—An Indian Deed.—Meaning of Pennypack. —Rev. Elias Keach.—The First Baptism.—Lower Dublin Church Constituted.—Change of Calendar.—Quarterly Meetings.—Conference Meetings.—Decease of Rev. Thomas Dungan.—Rev. John Watts. . 17

CHAPTER II.—1691-1700.—Keithians.—Baptists and Liberty of Conscience—Rev. Thomas Killingsworth.—William Davis.—Preaching at Cold Spring.—A Catechism and Confession of Faith.—Quaker Baptists.—Mennonites.—Rev. E. Keach Returns to England.—Rev. Morgan Edwards and Baptist History.—First Baptist Church of Philadelphia Organized.—Prominence of John Holme.—Rev. Hanserd Knollys.—Barbadoes Storehouse.—Baptists and Presbyterians.—Separation.—Meeting in a Brewhouse.—Baptists and Episcopalians.—Christ Church. 27

CHAPTER III.—1701-1710.—The Seventh-Day Baptists.—An Emigrant Church.—Laying on of Hands and Singing.—Death of Rev. John Watts.—First Baptist Church and the Keithians.—A Constant Supply of Ministers.—The Philadelphia Baptist Association.—More Ministers. 39

CHAPTER IV.—1711-1720.—Dissensions.—Ruling Elders.—The Montgomery Church Organized.—William Thomas.—Tunkers in Germantown.— . . . . - 48

CHAPTER V. 1721-1730.—Death of Samuel Jones and Abel Morgan. —An Educated Ministry.—Thomas Hollis.—Harvard College.—Order in Church services.—Careful Reception of Ministers from Abroad.—The Fourth Commandment.—Marrying an Unbeliever.—Forfeit of Office and Membership in the Church.—Letters of Churches to the Association.—Closed Doors.—Tunker Church Organized.—George Eaglesfield.—Benjamin Griffith Ordained.—Reception of Members from Great Britain.—Rev. Jenkin Jones at Pennypack.—William Kinnersley.—Joseph Eaton Ordained.—Church Letters not Granted.—Laying on of Hands in Ordination.—Fraternal Correspondence with London.—The First Circular Letter. 55

CHAPTER VI.—1731-1740.—The Baptist Meeting-House Built.—
Assistance Needed.—Baptists and the Romanists.—Church of England Demands the Baptist Property.—Fail to get it.—William Kinnersley Dies.—Samuel Jones and Samuel Stillman.—Rev. George Whitefield Arrives.—A Spiritual Man.—The Rev. Jenkin Jones.—Various Questions.—Association Records.—Catechetical Instruction.—Fifty-six Baptized.—Denominational Growth Slow.   63

CHAPTER VII.—1741-1750.—Philadelphia Confession of Faith.—
Subjects of Articles.—Ebenezer Kinnersley Ordained.—Doubts on Whitefield's Preaching.—Electricity.—Joseph Eaton's Defection.—First Baptist Church Reconstituted.—Groundless Question.—Constituent Members.—The Southampton Baptist Church.—George Eaton and Peter P. Vanhorn.—Abraham Levering.—First Records of the Association.—Benjamin Griffith.—Power and Duty of an Association.—Death of Rev. Joseph Wood.—Trouble with the Pennypack Property.—Death of Rev. Joseph Eaton.—Rev. Isaac Eaton and Hopewell Academy.—Moderator's Name First Given.—Nathaniel Jenkins. . 67

CHAPTER VIII.—1751-1760.—Feeble Churches Supplied with Preaching.—Ministers Ordained at the Association.—Other Associations Organized.—George Eaton Called to the Ministry.—Ebenezer Kinnersley, a Professor in the University of Pennsylvania.—New Britain Church Constituted.—John Davis Ordained.—The Pioneer Baptists of Maryland.—Ordination Certificate.—First Latin Grammar School.—Hopewell Academy.—Association's Jubilee.—Talents Developed.—Ministerial Supply.—Doctrinal Sermon.—Meagre Records.—First Church Pulpit Supplied.—Application to England for a Pastor.—Death of Rev. Jenkin Jones.—His Legacy.—Dissenting Ministers Permitted to Solemnize Marriages.—Mount Moriah Cemetery.—Rev. Morgan Edwards Invited from England.—First Fruit of the Hopewell School.—Rev. John Gano.—Rev. Samuel Stillman.—Various Occurrences. . . 74

CHAPTER IX.—1761-1763.—A New Era.—Rev. Morgan Edwards Arrives.—Dr. G. Weed's Self-Esteem.—Excommunicated for Drunkenness.—Supervision of the Membership.—Morgan Edwards Prominent. Association's Letter to England.—Need of Books.—First Table of Statistics.—Brown University Projected.—Morgan Edwards the Projector.—Educational Growth.—New Meeting-House in Philadelphia.—St. Michael's Lutheran Church.—Sound of the Organ.—Resignation of Rev. P. P. Vanhorn.—The City's Seal to Ordination Certificates.—George Eaton.—Samuel Jones Baptized.—Licensed to Preach.—Copy of the License.—Ordained.—Place of Worship Occupied.—Mr. Whitefield's Church.—Samuel Jones Pastor at Pennypack.—A Prerogative of the Ministry.—Wearing a Master's Gown.—Rev. Stephen Watts.—Ordination of Deacons. 82

CHAPTER X.—1764-1770.—The Sisters Allowed to Vote.—Ruling Elders.—Fraternal Associational Correspondence.—Warren Association Organized.—Letter from Philadelphia.—Rhode Island College and Morgan Edwards.—Death of Rev. Benjamin Griffith.—First Commencement of Brown University.—Minutes First Printed.—Northern Liberties Church.—Persecutions.—Philadelphia Association to the Rescue.—Sufferings at Ashfield.—New Meeting-House at Pennypack. 93

CHAPTER XI.—1771-1775—A Decade of Trial.—Rev. Morgan Edwards Resigns.—Rev. Samuel Stillman Chosen Pastor.—Did not Accept.—Northern Liberty Church in the Association.—The Missionary Spirit.—Morgan Edwards an Evangelist.—Rev. William Rogers Ordained.—Last Sermon of Rev. Issac Eaton.—Divine Blessing.—John Levering.—Laying on of Hands.—Rev. Ebenezer Kinnersley Resigns his Professorship.—Death and Burial of Mr. Kinnersley.—Memorial Window.—Persecutions of Baptists.—Association Meeting twice a Year. —Academy at Pennypack.—Burgiss Allison.—Carpenters' Hall.— Continental Congress.—Rev. Isaac Backus.—Diary of Backus in Philadelphia.—Committee of Grievances in the Association.—Meeting in Carpenters' Hall.—Address by Rev. James Manning.—Massachusetts Delegates Unfriendly.—Baptists and Soul Liberty.—Prejudiced Opinion of John Adams.—Committee Determined.—Printed Documents.— Fasting and Prayer.—Rev. William Rogers Resigned. . . . 102

CHAPTER XII.—1776-1780.—The Ever Memorable 1776.—Declaration of Independence.—Association at Scotch Plains.—Days of Humiliation.—Independence Hall.—Baptists on the Side of the Colonies.— Rev. William Rogers a Chaplain.—Ingenuity of Burgiss Allison.—Rev. John Pitman.—Patriotism of the Pennypack Church.—No Association in 1777.—Philadelphia Church in Distress.—Rev. James Manning.— Diary of Manning in Philadelphia.—Price of Board.—Letter to Revs. Still and Miller—Rev. John Gano Called.—Windows Filled with Boards.—Gano's Reply.—Call Repeated.—Elhanan Winchester Chosen. —An Unfortunate Move.—Rev. David Jones.—First Hundred Years. 118

CHAPTER XIII.—1781-1782.—Apostacy of Winchester.—Protest.— Council Called.—Advice of Association.—Lawsuit for Property.— Excommunicated.—Address from the Church.—Winchester's Death.— Baptisterion.—Rev. James Manning.—Issues of the War.—Messenger Association in Session.—Met at Sunrise.—Success of American Arms. —Statistics of Churches.—Out of the Ordeal.—Petition the General Assembly.—Ask to be Incorporated.—Desire President Manning.— Rev. Thomas Ustick Settled.—Sketch of Ustick.—Circulation of the Bible.—Brown University Commended.—Honeywell School Fund.— John Honeywell's Will. 130

CHAPTER XIV.—1788-1790.—Scruples Concerning Laying on of Hands.—Keep the Ordinances as Delivered.—Montgom.ry County Formed.—President Manning and Philadelphia Baptists.—The First Doctor of Divinity.—Lord's Supper, and Scattered Members.—Loyalty to the Colonies.—Pennypack Church Incorporated.—The Temperance Question.—A Baptist Hymn Book.—Rev. Samuel Jones, a Doctor of Divinity.—Singing Avoided.—Authorized Tunes.—Rev. Wm. Rogers Appointed to a Professorship.—Plain Furniture.—Roxborough Church Organized.—Abolition of Slavery.—Old Meeting-House at Roxborough. 139

CHAPTER XV.—1791-1800.—Rev. Curtis Gilbert.—Chestnut Hill.— Rev. Thomas Ainger.—Death of President Manning.—Sunday-school Society.—Regulation of Youth.—Destitute Orphans.—Notification of Members Received.—Soppression of Plays.—Recommendation or Dismission.—Joseph Keen.—Home Missions.—Death of Morgan Edwards.—Rev. Wiliam White Ordained.—Yellow Fever.—Rev. Rev. Thomas Ustick.—A Second Church.—Association Chartered.— Churches Dropped.—Chains Across the Street.—Death of George Washington.—Rev. Thomas Fleeson at Roxborough.—A Forward Movement.—A Feeble Folk.—Missionary Efforts. . . . 147

CHAPTER XVI.—1801-1806.—A New Era of Growth.—Measures Toward an African Church.—Letters from Carey.—A Missionary Spirit.—Baptisms on a Week-day.—Shade Trees at the Baptisterion.— Joseph S. Walter.—Holy Spirit Poured Out.—Second Baptist Church Constituted.—Moderator Should be a Member.—A Masonic Lodge Room Used for Religious Worship.—The Second Baptist Meeting-House Dedicated.—Death of Thomas Ustick.—Blockley Baptist Church Constituted.—Build a Meeting-House.—Singing Led by Precentors.— Christians in the Choirs.—Rev. William White, Pastor of the Second Church.—Licentiates' Names.—Rev. William Staughion in Philadelphia.—Crowded Congregation.—New Meeting-House at Lower Dublin.—First Baptist Meeting-House Enlarged.—Four Sermons on Sunday.—Hoartio Gates Jones, D.D.—Churches Lighted by Candles.— Heated by Wood Stoves.—Blank Forms of Letters of Dismission.—First Collection for Foreign Missions—Number of Members Necessary to Form a Church.—Valid Baptism.—Christian Missions.—Rev. John Rutter Excluded.—Invalid Marriages. 157

CHAPTER.X VII.—1807-1810.—City Pastors Residing in the Country. Frankford Baptist Church Constituted.—Meeting-House Erected.— Centennial Anniversary of Philadelphia Association.—Chronological List of Churches.—Second Baptist Church Incorporated.—John P. Crozer.—Wayside Efforts.—Third Baptist Church Constituted.—Imposition of Hands.—Fifteen Hundred Dollars and Parsonage.—Close Supervision and Strict Discipline.—Prohibition of Society Funerals.— First African Baptist Church Constituted.—House for Baptismal Occasions.—Missionary Society Extending its Labors. . . 169

CHAPTER XVIII.—1811-1815.—Growth of the City Westward.— Sansom Street Baptist Church Organized.—Dr. Staughton Ssttled as Pastor.—Collections at the Lord's Supper.—Rev. John E. Peckworth.— Rev. David Jones, Jr , at Frankford.—Rev. Henry Holcombe, D. D., Pastor First Baptist Chnrch, Philadelphia.—Missionary Spirit.—A Princeton Student Baptized.—A Scriptural Right to Baptize.—Rev. John King.—Baptist Orphan Society.—Emporium of Baptist Influence. First American Missionaries.—Philadelphia Baptist Society for Foreign Missions.—A Consecrated Spot.—Triennial Convention.—Names of Delegates.—Death of Dr. Samuel Jones.—Sunday-Schools Organized. —History of the First Church Bible School.—Historical Address by Judge Hanna. 178

CHAPTER XIX.—CONCLUSION.—Prominent Incidents and Persons. —Rev. Jacob Griggs.—Rev. William E. Ashton.—Rev. Wm. Wilson. —Rev. J. C. Murphy.—Defection of William White.—Rev. James McLaughlin.—The Fourth Baptist Church Constituted.—Meeting-House Erected.—The Latter-Day Luminary.—First Theological Seminary—Graduating Class.—Columbian University.—A Few Honored Names.—J. H. Kennard.—Daniel Dodge.—William J. Brantley.— Rufus Babcock.—K. A. Fleischman.—George B. Ide.—James M. Linnard.—Joseph Taylor.—Wilson Jewell.—David Jayne.—Franklin Lee.—W. H. Richards.—Thomas Wattson.—J. P. Sherborne. . 189

PREFACE.

This work, on the Early Baptists of Philadelphia, does not claim to exhaust all that might be said about them, nor does it profess to be infallible on every point. The material for it has been collected and prepared amidst the pressing duties of pastoral and other denominational work, and it is presented to the public in this form, in the hope that, at no very distant day, an abler pen may do more ample justice to the memory and work of the men who in the past have rendered such valuable service to the cause of truth in these parts of our great and growing country.

In publishing a few of the earlier chapters in the NATIONAL BAPTIST the following incident was given:—

In an old Welsh Bible belonging to the Lower Dublin Baptist Church of this city (now in the collection of the American Baptist Historical Society), printed in London, in 1678, is the following record:—

Sarah, daughter of Peter Davies, Baptist minister, Dolau, Radnorshire, South Wales, came over and settled in Penepec, in the year 1680, and through her letters, induced to follow her, George Eaton, John Eaton and Jane Eaton, together with Samuel Jones, a preacher in Dolau, and they were amongst those who founded the church in Penepec, in 1688. This Bible was brought over by them and has been preserved ever since in the Penepec Church, now called Lower Dublin. May God continue to bless and prosper this dear old church.

October 12th, 1869. THOMAS PRICE, Aberdare, Wales.

Dr. Price made the above entry, while on a visit to this country in 1869. Meeting with it at Lower Dublin, and wishing to determine the correctness of it, Dr. Price was written to for his authority. He replied promptly, and sent very full notes from a lecture prepared with great care for the Welsh in America. He says, "I was then

(1869) assisted as to dates by the late Rev. William Roberts, L.L.D., the first pastor of Rev. P. L. Davies, of New York. Dr. Roberts had spent a life-time in gathering together material for a Baptist History, but I regret that he is now dead, and I fear that his great labors, to a large extent, will be lost. I am not able now to give you documentary proof of any date, but I had implicit confidence in him."

A thorough examination into the above, warrants the statement, that it is entirely without foundation, and therefore it is expunged from the body of this work.

Praying the blessing of heaven upon this humble contribution to the historical literature of our honored denomination, it is sent forth upon its mission of interest to those who may peruse its pages.

THE

EARLY BAPTISTS OF PHILADELPHIA.

CHAPTER I.—1684–1690.

PHILADELPHIA FOUNDED.—RELIGIOUS LIBERTY.—WELSH PARENTAGE. —ORIGIN OF BAPTISTS.—JOHN HOLME PURCHASES LAND.—REV. THOMAS DUNGAN.—COLD SPRING CHURCH.—BUCKS AND PHILADELPHIA COUNTIES.—WILLIAM PENN AND THOMAS DUNGAN.—AN ENGLISH BAPTIST.—A CELEBRATED SPRING.—PERSECUTION IN WALES.—SETTLEMENT AT PENNYPACK.—AN INDIAN DEED.—MEANING OF PENNYPACK.—REV. ELIAS KEACH.—THE FIRST BAPTISM.— LOWER DUBLIN CHURCH CONSTITUTED.—CHANGE OF CALENDER.— QUARTERLY MEETINGS.—CONFERENCE MEETINGS.—DECEASE OF REV. THOMAS DUNGAN.—REV. JOHN WATTS.

MUCH that is exceedingly interesting clusters around the early history of the Baptists of Philadelphia, coeval as it is with that of the city itself. William Penn received the charter of Pennsylvania March 14th, 1681. He did not, however, reach the site now occupied by the city until the early part of November, 1682. An old record of a meeting held at Shackamaxon, on the 8th of November, says: "At this time Governor Penn and a number of Friends arrived here, and erected a city called Philadelphia, about half a mile from Shackamaxon."

The frame of Government as established, was in the main on the broad platform of Religious Liberty. The thirty-fifth law of the statutes as agreed upon May 5th, 1682, declared "That all persons living in this Province, who confess and acknowledge the Almighty and Eternal God to be the Creator, upholder and ruler of the world, and

B

that hold themselves obliged in conscience to live peaceably and justly in civil society, shall in no ways be molested or prejudiced for their religious persuasion or practice in matters of faith and worship, nor shall they be compelled at any time to frequent or maintain any religious worship, place or ministry whatever."

The Welsh Baptist historian (J. Davis) claims that "Wales is to be considered as the parent of the Baptist denomination in Pennsylvania."

The question is sometimes asked, where did the Baptists start from? Those who know no better say from Roger Williams, in Rhode Island. Philadelphia Baptists trace their origin to Wales, and the Welsh Baptists have traced their history back to A. D. 63. From that date to Christ in Palestine, it is not difficult to track out the New Testament doctrines and practices which still distinguish us as the followers of Jesus.

Between Penn's reception of the charter and his arrival in Philadelphia, the sale of land had commenced. In his letter to Philip Ford, dated May 22d, 1682, the name of John Holme is given as one of the first purchasers of land in this city. It is not improbable that he is the same man of whom Morgan Edwards says, "In the year 1686, one John Holmes, who was a Baptist, arrived and settled in the neighborhood." He was the ancestor of the Holme family, for many years associated with the Holmesburg Baptist Church of this city, and of Rev. J. Stanford Holme, D. D., of New York.

Rev. Thomas Dungan was the first Baptist minister who located in these parts. He came with a colony from Rhode Island, where he had been a member of the First Baptist Church of Newport, and settled, in 1684, at Cold Spring, in Bucks county, about three miles north of Bristol. Here he founded a Baptist church—the first one west of New England, except one in Charleston, S. C., constituted in 1683. As the exact line between Bucks and Philadelphia counties was not fixed until April 1st, 1685, as Dungan naturally visited this city before finally locating where he did, and as the Cold Spring interest "was, in the end, absorbed by the" Lower Dublin Church, of this city, the history of this first church in Pennsylvania legitimately belongs to that of Philadelphia. Between Penn and Dungan there may have been a friendly, though, necessarily, a short intimacy, as the former returned to England August 12th, 1684. The reasons for this supposed intimacy may be given. Admiral Penn, the father of William, Benedict[*] says, was an "English Baptist." William Penn himself, though a Quaker, entertained strong Baptist sentiments. In enacting laws for the government of Pennsylvania he recognized those rights for which Baptists have so earnestly contended, and which had already been incorporated by Roger Williams in the statutes of Rhode Island.

Rev. Thomas Dungan was born in Ireland. Owing to the bitter hostility to Baptists, under the reign of Charles II., he came to America, only to find in New England the same spirit of persecution. Coming thence to Philadelphia, his settlement at Cold Spring was not accidental. Here is a most remarkable spring, throwing out a strong and steady stream of clear, cold water, whose temperature is the same all the year round. It is thought by some to possess qualities of great medicinal value. Tradition tells us that the Indians were accustomed to assemble about it twice a year, and bring their sick to enjoy its healing qualities. At the change of the seasons, the time of their semi-annual gathering, a mist would form over the spring, which, to the Indian's fancy, assumed the shape of a spirit, whose good

---

[*] History of the Baptists, page 595.

will they desired to enjoy. In selling their lands to William Penn, when speaking of their value, it is not impossible they spoke of this spring, located in a most beautiful spot on the banks of the Delaware. So, when Dungan came to purchase land, desiring a quiet region, where he could end his days peacefully, Penn, from the love he bore to the Baptists, and for his sympathy for those who had come out of terrible persecutions, offered him this celebrated place.

With the church at Cold Spring it is supposed the father of the celebrated Dr. Benjamin Rush, one of the signers of the Declaration of Independence, was associated.[*] He was buried in the graveyard adjoining this church. At that time Philadelphia had a population of 2500 persons.

Upon the restoration of Charles II. to the throne of Great Britain, commenced a series of fearful persecutions, in which the Baptists suffered a large share. In Wales, for twenty-eight years, during his reign, "they had to meet," says Davis, "in the most secret places by night, somewhere in the woods, or on the Black mountain, or the rough rock. They were obliged to change the place every week, that their enemies might not find them out. Often the friends of the infernal foe diligently sought them, but found them not. While the wolves were searching in one mountain, the lambs were sheltering under the rock of another. But, notwithstanding all their care and prudence, they were sometimes caught, and most unmercifully whipped and fined. Their cattle and household furniture were seized to pay the fines and expenses of the executioners of the law. The safest place they ever found was in the woods, under a large rock, called Darren Ddu, or the Black Rock. It is a most dreadful steep, and the roughest place we have ever seen."

---

[*] See preface to Century Minutes of Philadelphia Baptist Association.

So great was the hostility of the public authorities that the Baptists were not permitted to bury their dead in the graveyards. They humbly petitioned the King for protection, concluding their appeal thus:—

> O, King, we dare not walk the streets, and we are abused even in our own houses. If we pray to God with our families, we are threatened to be hung. Some of us are stoned almost to death, and others are imprisoned for worshipping God according to the dictates of their own consciences and the rule of his word.

This plea was disregarded, and the persecutions from 1660 to 1688 were most bitter. During all this time the annual meetings of the Baptist Association were not held, but the opening of Pennsylvania was a source of hope to these distressed children of God, and two years before the persecution in Wales ended, by reason of its bitterness, several members of the Baptist Church of Dolau, with their families, sailed for America. Arriving in Philadelphia in 1686, they settled on the banks of the Pennypack Creek. These, with others, subsequently constituted the Pennypack, now Lower Dublin, Baptist Church, of this city. Its ancient records state:—

> By the good providence of God, there came certain persons out of Radnorshire in Wales, and over into this province of Pennsylvania, and settled in the township of Dublin, in the county of Philadelphia, viz.: John Eatton, George Eatton, and Jane, his wife, Samuel Jones and Sarah Eatton, who had been baptized upon confession of faith and received into the communion of the church of Christ, meeting in the parishes of Llandewi and Nantmel, in Radnorshire, Henry Gregory being chief pastor. Also John Baker, who had been baptized, and a member of a congregation of baptized believers in Kilkenny, in Ireland, Christopher Blackwell, pastor, was, by the providence of God, settled in the township aforesaid. In the year 1687 there came one Samuel Vaus, out of England, and settled near the aforesaid township, and went under the denomination of a Baptist, and was so taken to be.

It was, however, shortly after learned that he had never been baptized, and when confronted on the subject by the pastor, he acknowledged his imposition, and ceased to be one of the church.

It is to these lands, and, perhaps, to some of the very Christians named in the foregoing, that the following copy of an Indian deed refers:—

"I, Richard Mettamicont, Owner of ye Land on both sides of Pemmapecca Creek, on the River Delaware, do hereby acknowledge yt of my own accord and freewill, I have offer{d} given and disposed of, and by these presents do give and dispose of all my Land, situated as above mentioned, for me and my Heires forever, unto William Penn, Proprietary and Govern{r} of ye Province of Pennsilvania, &c., his Heirs and Assignes forever, In consideration of wch I confess to have received by Ord{r} of ye said Govern{r}, one match coat, one pair of stockings and one shert; And I do now promise never to molest or trouble any Christians so called, settled upon any part of ye aforesaid Land, by authority of Governour Penn. Witness my hand and seal, Philadelphia, ye 7th ye 4th month (June), 1684.

RICHARD + METTAMICONT, [L.S.]
His mark.

Sign'd, seald and delivered in ye presence of
PHILIP TH. LEHNMANN,
TRYALL HOLME.

Indorsed partly by Penn.—" Rich. Mettamicont Deed for Lands on both sides of Pemmapecka Creek."

The word Pemmapecca, in the above, leads us to say the stream of that name was thus called at first, then Pennepek. Now it is generally written Pennypack. It means, *a pond, lake or bay; water not having a current.* To avoid confusion, we hereafter speak of the Pennypack Church under its present name of Lower Dublin or Pennypack interchangeably.

About the same time, Elias Keach, a son of the celebrated Baptist minister, Rev. Benjamin Keach, of London, settled in Lower Dublin. He was born in England in 1666, so that he was only twenty years of age when he came to this country. Morgan Edwards says of him:—

On his landing he dressed in black, and wore a band in order to pass for a minister. The project succeeded to his wishes, and many people resorted to hear the young London divine. He performed well enough till he had advanced pretty far in the sermon. Then, stopping short, he looked like a man astonished. The audience concluded he had been seized with a sudden disorder; but on asking what the matter was, received from him a confession of the imposture, with tears in his eyes, and much trembling. Great was his distress, though it ended happily; for from this time he dated his conversion. He heard there was a Baptist minister at Cold Spring, in Bucks county, between Bristol and Trentown. To him did he repair to seek counsel and comfort; and by him was he baptized and ordained.

The site of his baptism is one of the most beautiful, for such a purpose, to be found along the Delaware river. The sloping bank with its pebbly bottom, and the bend in the river, giving a view up and down for miles, is very fine. From then until the present, this same location has frequently been the scene of Bible baptism. The Christian Church, of Tullytown, one mile above, baptize their candidates here. After his baptism, Mr. Keach at once devoted himself to the work of the ministry at Pennypack. Success attended him, and on November 21, 1687, he baptized Joseph Ashton, Jane Ashton, his wife, Wm. Fisher and John Watts.

So far as known, this is the first record of a baptism in what is now Philadelphia, and it probably took place in the Pennypack Creek, at a charming point, which, to this day, is used by this venerable church for the same purpose. Of this spot the late Rev. William T. Brantly, D. D., wrote in 1829:—

A flat rock, which projects into the stream at a certain point, and leaves an easy slope into the water, has been for a series of years the platform on which the administrator of Baptism has stood to propound the way of truth to the surrounding multitude, and from which he has conducted into the yielding elements below him, the placid forms of new converts.

The church at Lower Dublin was constituted in January, 1688, with twelve members. The account of this event is given in the church records thus:—

Sometime after, about the 11th month (January, 1687-8), by the advice of Elias Keach and with the aforesaid baptized persons' consent, a day was set apart to seek God by fasting and prayer, in order to form ourselves into a church state. Whereupon Elias Keach was accepted and received for our pastor, and we sat down in communion at the Lord's table. Also at the same time Samuel Vaus was chosen, and by Elias Keach, with laying on of hands, was ordained to be a deacon.

When the above record was made the year began on March 25th. March was then called the first month, and that is why September, October, November and December were called respectively, as their names in Latin signify, the seventh, eighth, ninth and tenth months. The eleventh month, spoken of above, would of course be January. In 1752 the calendar was changed from the old style to the arrangement as at present. Previous to this change it was proper to say that the church was organized in 1687, but when the change was made "the eleventh month, 1687," became the first month or January, 1688. This change is the reason why Morgan Edwards gives, in brackets, the double date of 1687-8.

Well has Dr. J. R. Murphy, in his memoir of Rev. J. M. Challis, a subsequent pastor at Lower Dublin, said:—

Thus this old church and mother of churches was organized during the very incipiency of the settlement, while yet the homes of its members were in the midst of the Indians' hunting grounds. The Neshammies and Shackamaxons were still lingering in the old homes along the Delaware, and the echo of the Indian war-song had scarcely died away when the songs of praise to God arose from an assembled church of Christ, and the wilderness and the solitary place was glad.

Mr. Keach extended his ministerial labors into New Jersey, to Trenton, Burlington, Middletown, Cohansey and Salem. He frequently preached in Philadelphia, Chester, and other places. At that time all the Baptists of Philadelphia and New Jersey were regarded as general members of this church. Morgan Edwards says:—

They were all one church, and Pennepeck the centre of union, where as many as could, met to celebrate the memorials of Christ's death; and for the sake of distant members they administered the ordinance quarterly at Burlington, Cohansey, Chester and Philadelphia; which quarterly meetings have since transformed into three yearly meetings and an association.

Thus, for some time, continued their Zion with lengthened cords till the brethren in remote parts set about forming themselves into distinct churches, which began in 1689 and continued until these late years. By these detachments Pennepeck was reduced to narrow bounds, but yet abides among the churches as a mother in the midst of many daughters.

The distance of the above-named places from Lower Dublin, and the increase in the number of baptized believers, led to the organization of churches at Middletown in 1688, Piscataway in 1689, Cohansey in 1690, and Philadelphia in 1698.

Dr. Benedict well says of Mr. Keach, "that he may be considered as the chief apostle among the Baptists in these parts of America." Visiting these numerous places in that early day necessitated his absence from Lower Dublin frequently, but the little band of disciples kept up each week "meetings for Conference," wherein "every brother might have opportunity to exercise what gifts God had been pleased to bestow on them for the edification of one another." In this way brethren gifted in prayer and exhortation were brought out, and the church enabled always to have within her own fold those upon whom she could depend in the absence of her pastor.

Differences arose in the church relative to laying on of hands after baptism, and upon other matters of doctrine and practice, so that in 1689 Mr. Keach resigned the pastorate and devoted himself to preaching the gospel in various parts of Pennsylvania and New Jersey.

The year that witnessed the constitution of the Lower Dublin Church was also signalized by the death of Rev. Thomas Dungan.

Of this venerable father (says Morgan Edwards, in 1770) I can learn no more than that he came from Rhode Island, about the year 1684. That he and his family settled at Cold Spring, where he gathered a church, of which nothing remains but a graveyard and the names of the families which belonged to it, viz.: the *Dungans, Gardeners, Woods, Doyles,* etc. That he died in 1688 and was buried in said graveyard. That his children were five sons and four daughters, who formed connections with families by the names of Wing of Rhode Island; Drake, West, Richards, Doyle and Kerrels. To mention the names, alliance and offspring of these, would tend towards an endless genealogy. Sufficeth it that the Rev. Thomas Dungan, the first Baptist minister in the province, now existeth in a progeny of between six and seven hundred.

Mr. Dungan must have been a man far advanced in years, as the Minutes of the Lower Dublin Church, in speaking of him as baptizing Elias Keach, call him "an *ancient* disciple and teacher among the Baptists."

December 10, 1690, Rev. John Watts assumed the pastorate at Lower Dublin. He was born in Leeds, Kent County, England, baptized by Rev. Elias Keach, November 21, 1687, and was a constituent of the church, whose pastorate he now filled. He was a man of decided talents as a preacher and writer, and most earnestly contended for the faith delivered *once for all* to the saints. He was, as we shall see, destined to take a prominent part in the earliest history and founding of the First Baptist Church of this city. His settlement as pastor at Lower Dublin was the last important event in the first decade of Baptist history in Philadelphia.

CHAPTER II.—1691-1700.

KEITHIANS.—BAPTISTS AND LIBERTY OF CONSCIENCE.—REV. THOMAS KILLINGSWORTH.—WILLIAM DAVIS.—PREACHING AT COLD SPRING. —A CATECHISM AND CONFESSION OF FAITH.—QUAKER BAPTISTS.— MENNONITES.—REV. E. KEACH RETURNS TO ENGLAND.—REV. MORGAN EDWARDS AND BAPTIST HISTORY.- FIRST BAPTIST CHURCH OF PHILADELPHIA ORGANIZED.—PROMINENCE OF JOHN HOLME.— REV. HANSERD KNOLLYS.—BARBADOES STOREHOUSE.—BAPTISTS AND PRESBYTERIANS.—SEPARATION.—MEETING IN A BREWHOUSE. —BAPTISTS AND EPISCOPALIANS.—CHRIST CHURCH.

THE closing decade of the seventeenth century was not without interest among the Baptists of this city. In 1691 a division arose among the Quakers, "touching the sufficiency of what every man has within himself, for the purpose of his own salvation." Some denied that sufficiency, and consequently magnified the external Word, Christ, etc. These were headed by the celebrated George Keith, and, therefore, were called Keithians. They were about fifty in number. He issued several articles.

1. To inform the world of the principles of the Separate Quakers.
2. To fix the blame of separation on the opposite party.
3. To complain of the unfair treatment, slanders, fines, imprisonments, and other species of persecution, which they endured from their brethren.

"Whether these complaints," says Morgan Edwards, "be just or not, is neither my business nor inclination to determine. If just, the Quakers have also shown that every sect would persecute, had they but power. I know of but one exception to this satirical remark, and that is the Baptists; they have had civil power in their hands in Rhode Island government, and yet have never abused it in this manner, their enemies themselves being judges. And it is remarkable that John Holmes, Esq., the only Baptist magistrate in Philadelphia at the time referred to, refused to act with the Quaker magistrates, against the Keithians, alleging that it was a religious dispute, and, therefore, not fit for a civil court. Nay, he openly blamed the court, held at Philadelphia, December 6-12, 1692, for refusing to admit the exceptions which the prisoners made to their jury. However, the Keithian Quakers soon declined; their head deserted them and went over to the Episcopalians. Some followed him thither; some returned to the Penn Quakers; and some went to other societies. Nevertheless, many persisted in the separation, particularly at Upper Providence, at Philadelphia, at Southampton, and at Lower Dublin. The Keithian Quakers who kept together at Philadelphia, built a meeting-house in 1692. Of these two public persons were baptized in 1697, by Rev. Thomas Killingsworth, of Cohansey. Their names were William Davis and Thomas Rutter. The first joined Pennepeck; the other kept preaching in Philadelphia, where he baptized one Henry Bernard Hoster, Thomas Peart, and seven others whose names are not on record. These nine persons united in communion June 12th, 1698, having Thomas Rutter to be their minister."

Rev. Mr. Killingsworth was an English Baptist minister. Having removed to this country in the year 1686 he began preaching the gospel in the vicinity of Piscataway, New Jersey, and aided in founding the Baptist Church of that name. About 1692 he settled near Salem, in the same State, and was the first pastor of the Cohansey Baptist Church. He was a man of talent, energy and good sense.

The aforenamed William Davis became a troubler in Zion. He had been a Quaker preacher, then a Keithian, and finally a Baptist. He held Sabellian views, and was so pronounced in them as to make himself a subject of discipline. Rev. John Watts wrote a book entitled *Davis Disabled*, in reply to the heresies of his parishoner. Davis was finally excluded from the Lower Dublin Church. At this time, in the vicinity of Pennypack, there was a body of Keithians, one of whom, on September 27th, 1697, became a Baptist. To this party William Davis joined himself, and became their minister. In 1699 they received quite an accession to their number by baptism.

After the death of Rev. Thomas Dungan, Elias Keach and John Watts preached as often as possible at Cold Spring, about nine miles distant from Pennypack. In 1692, in the Minutes of the Pennypack Church, the names of five of the

Cold Spring members are given, among whom is Elizabeth, the widow of the late pastor, Mr. Dungan.

The varieties and phases of theological opinion prevalent, led the Baptists to feel the need of proper instruction in the true faith for their children and the church members. Mr. Watts was, therefore, requested to prepare a Catechism and Confession of Faith, which he did, and it was published in 1700.

The Keithian Quakers soon became convinced on the subject of baptism, and "ended in a kind of transformation of Keithian Baptists; they were also called Quaker Baptists, because they still retained the language, dress and manners of the Quakers." These again divided on the Sabbath question; some becoming Seventh-day while the others went among the First-day Baptists. A Confession of Faith was published by the Keithian Baptists in 1697. It consists chiefly of the Apostle's Creed. The additions are articles which relate to baptism by immersion, the Lord's Supper, distinguishing days and months by numerical names, "plainness of language and dress, not swearing, not fighting," etc.

In 1692 some Mennonite families settled in the neighborhood of Germantown and Frankford; and to these constant accessions were made of others who emigrated from Europe. The founder of this sect was Menno Simon, a German Baptist, who was born in Friesland, in 1505, and who died in Holstein in 1561. This body originally were strict immersionists. Their founder declared, "After we have searched diligently, we shall find no other baptism but dipping in the water, which is acceptable to God and approved in his word."

Rev. Elias Keach did not remain long to witness the growth of those principles he so earnestly advocated. In the spring of 1692 he embarked for England with his family, and became a celebrated and successful preacher in London. Hon. Horatio Gates Jones, of this city, who has rendered most valuable service to the denomination hereabouts in collecting facts and papers relating to our early history, says,* of this first Baptist pastor in the city of Philadelphia, after his return to England:—

He became pastor of a church, which he was instrumental in gathering, in Ayles Street, Goodman's-field, London, in April, 1693; and, so successful was he, that in February, 1694, he wrote to Rev. John Watts, that in nine months he had baptized about one hundred and thirty persons. He remained the pastor of that church until October 27, 1699, when he died, after a brief illness, in the thirty-fourth year of his age. His funeral sermon was preached by Rev. Nathaniel Wyles, and is entitled, *Death's Arrest, the Saint's Release.*

Mr. Keach wrote and published several works. First, Four sermons preached prior to 1694, in Pinner's Hall. Second, A Confession of Faith, Church Covenant, Discipline, etc. Third, Two sermons on *The Nature and Excellency of the Grace of Patience.* While in Pennsylvania, Mr. Keach married Mary Moore, a daughter of the Hon. Nicholas Moore, who was Chief Justice of Pennsylvania, and after whom the manor of Mooreland was named, he being the owner of that tract of land. They had an only daughter, Hannah, who married Revitt Harrison, of England, and had a son, John Elias Keach Harrison, who came to America about the year 1734, and lived at Hatborough, and was a member of the Baptist Church of Southampton, in Bucks county, Pa. The widow of Judge Moore, subsequently became the wife of John Holme, Esq., then of Philadelphia, but afterwards of Salem, N. J.

For the history of our denomination in this vicinity during these early times, we owe a debt of gratitude to Rev. Morgan Edwards. He gathered invaluable material for Baptist History. God be thanked for raising up such men. As a denomination we have not given due attention to our history. A Baptist who is thoroughly acquainted with the principles which he professes, is not often much concerned to trace his tenets through the different centuries of the Christian era. It is enough for him to find that the

---

* Historical sketch of the Lower Dublin Baptist Church, page 19.

doctrines he avows are distinctly expressed and commanded in the great commission of the Divine Redeemer, and that they were professed and preached by his inspired apostles. Yet he is not without testimony from, nor should he be uninterested in, ecclesiastical history, that from the days of the apostles to the present time, there were persons who held and advocated the principles he maintains.

The church at Lower Dublin was in what was then known as the county of Philadelphia. Yet this decade was not to close ere a Baptist church in the city was organized. Of this movement Morgan Edwards says :—

> In the year 1686, one John Holmes, who was a Baptist, arrived and settled in the neighborhood. He was a man of property and learning, and, therefore, we find him in the magistracy of the place in 1691, and was the same man who refused to act with the Quaker magistrates against the Keithians. He died Judge of Salem Court. In 1696, John Farmer and his wife, arrived; they belonged to the church of Rev. Hanserd Knollys. In 1697, one Joseph Todd and Rebecca Woosoncroft, came to the same neighborhood, who belonged to a Baptist church in Limmington, in Hampshire, England, whereof Rev. John Rumsay was pastor. The next year, one William Silverstone, William Elton and wife, and Mary Shephard, were baptized by John Watts. These nine persons, on the second Sunday of December, 1698, assembled at a house in *Barbadoes lot*, and coalesced into a church for the communion of saints, having Rev. John Watts to their assistance.

In addition to what Morgan Edwards says of the character of John Holme, we may add there are many illustrations of his ability, prominence and respectability as a man and a citizen. In a petition to the Governor and Council of this province, in 1691, relative " to the cove at the Blue Anchor to be laid out for a convenient harbor to secure shipping against ice or other danger of the winter, and that no person, for private gains or interest may incommode the public utility of a whole city "—immediately after the name of Humphrey Murray, who is spoken of as the " mayor," occurs the name of John Holme. The position of this name among many others being indicative of the prominence and the respectability of the man, while the subject of the petition is illustrative of his liberal views and excellent judgment. In 1696 he wrote a poem, entitled "A True Relation of the Flourishing State of Pennsylvania." It is published in the Bulletin of the Historical Society of Pennsylvania.*

BARBADOES STOREHOUSE.

Beginning with April, 1695, Rev. John Watts, pastor of the church at Lower Dublin, preached twice a month in the city of Philadelphia, in the Barbadoes storehouse, situated at the northwest corner of Second and Chestnut streets. The Presbyterians occupied this structure conjointly with the Baptists. The Presbyterians, however, were first to settle a pastor, the Rev. Jedediah Andrews, of New England. Coming from that part of our country where the Baptists were most bitterly persecuted, his love for them was not strong; hence he inaugurated measures to drive them out of the building they had occupied, in connection with the Presbyterians, for over three years.

---

*Volume 1, No. 13.

BAPTISTS AND PRESBYTERIANS. 33

In view of this conduct, the Baptists wrote to them the following courteous and Christian letter:—

To our dear and well beloved friends and brethren—Mr. Jedediah Andrews, John Green, Joshua Story and Samuel Richardson, and the rest of the Presbyterian judgment, belonging to the meeting in Philadelphia—the Church of Christ, baptized on confession of faith, over which Rev. John Watts is pastor, send salutation of grace, mercy and peace, from God our Father, and from our Lord Jesus Christ:—

DEARLY BELOVED: Having seriously and in the fear of God considered our duties of love to and bearing with one another, and receiving the weak in faith; and knowing that love, peace and unity tend much to the honor of Christ and Christianity, and to the conviction and conversion of sinners, and the comfort and establishment of believers, and being desirous of your company heavenward as far as may be, and as much as we can to heal the breach betwixt us, occasioned by our difference in judgment (none being yet perfect in knowledge), we have thought it necessary to make you this proposition following, for peace (as being the necessary term upon which we may safely, comfortably and peaceably hold Christian communion together in the things wherein we agree in the public worship of God and common duties of religion, as in prayer, preaching, praising God, reading and hearing the word), viz., we do freely confess and promise for ourselves that we can and do own and allow of all approved ministers, who are fitly qualified and sound in the faith, and of holy lives, to pray and preach in our assemblies. If you can also confess and promise for yourselves that you can and will own and allow of our approved ministers, who are fully qualified and sound in the faith, and of holy lives, to preach in your assemblies, that so each side may own, embrace and accept of each other as fellow brethren and ministers of Christ, and hold and maintain Christian communion and fellowship. Unto which proposition (that further disputes and vain janglings may be prevented) we shall desire, if you please, your plain and direct answer, that it may be left for us at Widow Elton's house in Philadelphia.

Subscribed in behalf of the rest of the congregation the 30th of 8th month (October), 1698.

JOHN WATTS, THOMAS BIBB,
SAMUEL JONES, THOMAS POTTS,
GEORGE EATON.

To the above letter a reply was returned by the Presbyterians, dated November 3, 1698, and signed by Rev. Jedediah Andrews, John Green, Samuel Richardson, David Giffing, Herbert Corry, John Vanlear and David Green, in

C

which they requested a conference at some time and place to be appointed by the Baptists, in order that they might agree upon what was to be done. The 19th of November was fixed for the consultation at the common meeting-house on the Barbadoes lot, and the notification was delivered to Mr. Andrews.

At the time appointed, Messrs. John Watts, Samuel Jones and Evan Morgan went to the city and were at the place of meeting, but no one came. Word was sent to Mr. Andrews, and his attendance was desired; but he excused himself on the pretext that he thought the time was the second day after, or the 22d inst. The three brethren waited all day, but in vain. Before leaving the building, they wrote a letter to the Presbyterians. After stating their disappointment in not meeting them for conference, they said:

> Considering what the desires of divers people are, and how they stand affected, and that we are not likely to receive an answer to our reasonable proposition, necessity constrains us to meet apart from you until such time as we receive an answer, and we are assured that you can own us so as we do you; though we still remain the same as before, and stand by what we have written.

The next day being Sunday, the Baptists met apart. "This," says Edwards, "was what the Presbyterians wanted, in reality, as more plainly appeared soon after, particularly in a letter directed to one Thomas Revell, of Burlington, and signed 'Jedediah Andrews,' wherein are these words: 'Though we have got the Anabaptists out of the house, yet our continuance there is uncertain, and therefore must think of building, notwithstanding our poverty.'"

The Baptists secured a place for worship near the *drawbridge*, known as Anthony Morris' Brewhouse. Here they continued their religious services unmolested for several years. This brewhouse was situated at what is now known as Dock and Water Streets. Nevertheless, the First Church was organized December 11, 1698, on the Barbadoes lot, as Morgan Edwards certifies.

During the progress of the difficulty relative to the occupancy of the storehouse, Rev. Thomas Clayton, Rector of Christ Church, sent a letter to the Baptists, inviting them to unite with the Church of England, where they could enjoy the comforts of a convenient house of worship, or if they could not accept the proposition, to state their reasons for rejecting it. The reply of the Baptists was eminently Christian in spirit, Baptistic in sentiment, and loyal in its adherence to the New Testament as our only rule in all matters of religious belief and practice. Persecution in the Barbadoes storehouse did not force the honored founders of our First Church into retaliation, nor did the alluring proffers of the Church of England tempt them to swerve in their loyalty to God's truth. Their reply to Rev. Thomas Clayton was as follows.—

Rev. Thomas Clayton.

SIR: Whereas we received a letter invitatory from you to return to your Church of England (dated Sept. 26, 1698), wherein you desire us to *send you in humility and without prejudice, the objections why we may not be united in one community, and withal that you doubt not but by the blessing and assistance of God, you will be able to show them to be stumbling-blocks made by our wills and not by our reason ;* and some of us, in behalf of the rest, having on the reception thereof given you a visit, and had discourse with you concerning some of the ceremonies of your church (about which you gave no satisfaction), we did not think that you expected any other answer from us; but in your late letter to John Watts, you signify that you have received no answer to your former letter. We, therefore, taking this into consideration, do signify, in answer to your aforesaid invitation and proposal, that to rend from a rightly constituted church of Christ is that which our souls abhor; and that love, peace and unity with all Christians, and concord and agreement in the true faith and worship of God are that which we greatly desire, and we should be glad if yourself or others would inform us whenever we err from the truth and ways of Christ. Nor are we averse to a reconciliation with the Church of England, provided it can be proved by the Holy Scriptures that her constitution, orders, officers, worship and service are of divine appointment, and not of human invention. And, since you yourself are the person that has given us the invitation, and hath promised to show us that *our objections are stumbling-blocks made by our wills and not by our reason,* and we understanding that our Lord Jesus Christ is the only Head, King, Lord and Lawgiver of his Church, whom all are bound to hear and obey under the severe penalty of an utter extermination from among the people of God, and that his laws and will are only to be found in and known by sacred Scriptures, which are the only supreme, sufficient and standing rule of all faith and worships, and not understanding the constitution of your church (with all the orders, officers, worship and service at this day in use and maintained therein) to be agreeable to and warranted thereby, hath been the cause of our separation from her, and is the objection we have to make, or the stumbling-block which lies in our way to such a union and communion as you desire. We, therefore, hope and expect, according to your promise, that you will endeavor its removal by showing us from Holy Scripture these two things, as absolutely necessary thereunto:

I. That the formation of your Church, with all the orders, officers, rites and ceremonies now in use and practiced therein, are of divine institution.

Particularly that the Church of Christ under the New Testament may consist or may be made up of a mixed multitude and their seed, even all that are members of a nation who are willing to go under the denomination of Christians, whether they are godly or ungodly, holy or profane.

That lords archbishops, and diocesan lords archbishops, such as are now in England, are of divine institution and appointment. That the government of the Church of Christ under the Gospel is prelatical according as it is practiced this day in your church, and that your ecclesiastical courts are of divine appointment. That particular churches or congregations, whether ministers or elders, who have power to receive persons with memberships, have not likewise authority (by Matthew 18: 15-18; 1 Corinthians 5) to execute Church censures and excommunication upon miscreants, swearers, liars, drunkards, adulterers, Jews, Atheists, etc.; but that it is by divine appointment that they must be presented to their ordinaries, and only proceeded against in our ecclesiastical courts. That the several offices of *deans, subdeans, chapters, archdeacons, prebendaries, chancellors, commissaries, officials, registers, canons, petty canons, vicars, chorals, appavitors, organists, vergers, singing men and boys, septins, epistlers, gospelers,* and such like offices and officers, of your church and ecclesiastical courts are of divine institution, or have any Scripture warrant to justify them, and to bear them harmless on the last day.

That unpreaching ministers may celebrate the sacraments by Scripture warrant. That their different apparel, in time of divine service, such as hoods, tippets, surplices, etc., are of divine institution or have any Scripture warrant in the New Testament.

That the manner of public service and liturgy of the Church of England, with the visitation of the sick, burial of the dead, churching of women, matrimony, etc., as now in use are of divine appointment. That the people ought, by the rule of God's word, only with the minister, to say the Confession, Lord's Prayer, and the Creed, and make such answers to the public prayers as are appointed in the Book of Common Prayer. That it is God's holy will and pleasure that saint's days or holy days should be kept and observed by Christians, according to the use of the Church of England.

That instruments of music are to be used in God's worship by the New Testament.

That infant baptism is a duty.

That pouring or sprinkling water is the proper way of baptizing.

That your manner of administering the sacraments, and signing with the cross in baptism, are of divine appointment.

These are some of the things we desire you to prove and make plain to us by the Holy Scriptures. But if the case is such that some or all of them cannot be, then the

II. Thing necessary to our reconciliation with your Church is, that you will give us clear and infallible proof from God's Holy Word, such as will bear us harmless in the last day, that our Lord Jesus Christ has given power and authority to any man, men, convocation, or synod, to make, constitute, and set up any other laws, orders, officers, rites, and ceremonies in his Church, beside those which he hath therein appointed, according as may from time to time seem convenient, and that we are bound in conscience towards God by the authority of his word to yield obedience thereunto, or whether it will not rather be a sore reflection upon the sufficiency of the Holy Scriptures, and a high defamation of the kingly and prophetical offices of Jesus Christ to suppose such a thing.

Thus we have *in humility and without prejudice sent our objections, and if you can, according to your letter, show them to be stumbling-blocks made by our wills and not by our reason,* we shall be very thankful, and you shall not find us obstinate, but ready to accept your invitation. But until you do so, and prove the constitution, orders, rites and ceremonies of your church to be of God, it is but reason that you should suspend all charge of *schism* against us, and desist from blaming us for our peaceful separation. Which is all, at present, from your loving friends, who desire information and unity among saints, and the churches' peace, that God may be glorified through our Lord Jesus Christ. Amen.

Subscribed by us, members of the general meeting, in behalf of all the rest, March 11th, 1699.

   JOHN WATTS,   JOSEPH WOOD,
  GEORGE EAGLESFIELD, SAMUEL JONES,
       THOMAS BIBB.

Owing to the interest which gathers about Christ Church and our own history, in view of the above, a picture of the church edifice, as it now stands on Second street above Market, is herewith given. It was erected in 1754.

CHRIST CHURCH.

CHAPTER III.—1701-1710.

THE SEVENTH-DAY BAPTISTS.—AN EMIGRANT CHURCH.—LAYING ON OF HANDS AND SINGING.—DEATH OF REV. JOHN WATTS.—FIRST BAPTIST CHURCH AND THE KEITHIANS.—A CONSTANT SUPPLY OF MINISTERS.—THE PHILADELPHIA BAPTIST ASSOCIATION.—MORE MINISTERS.

IN a previous article reference was made to the Seventh-Day Baptists. Morgan Edwards says, " They originated from the Keithian Baptists in 1700. Before that time, I can find but one Seventh-Day Baptist in Pennsylvania, viz., Mr. Abel Noble. He arrived, it is said, in 1684. His name is among the forty-eight who signed the reasons for the Keithian separation in 1691. By him was the first Keithian baptized in 1697, and by him were the rest gained over to the observance of the seventh day. I suppose, therefore, he may be called the father of them in this part of America." In the above, Mr. Edwards speaks of this sect, simply in these parts. It had existed in New England anterior to this time.

In 1701 the Pennypack Keithians, under the leadership of William Davis, having divided on the Sabbath question, "built a place of worship in Oxford Township." Their preacher subsequently left them and joined the Seventh-Day Baptists, their meeting-house was taken from them, and they were as sheep without a shepherd. Those who adhered to the first day Sabbath joined the Pennypack Baptist Church.

A society of Seventh-Day Baptists originated in the neighborhood, in 1701, by means of the efforts of Abel Noble. "In the year 1702," says Morgan Edwards, "they built a meeting-house on a lot given them by Thomas

Graves; but, having neglected to take a conveyance in due time, the Episcopalians have got both the lot and the house. On the lot they have built Oxford Church, and turned the Baptist meeting-house into a stable, while it stood, but now it is no more."

Notwithstanding the above statement, of the gift of the Oxford Church property, the ownership of it by the Episcopalians is legitimate, and cannot be disputed.

In 1701, an entire church, consisting of sixteen members, constituted in Pembrokeshire, South Wales, arrived in this country. Rev. Thomas Griffith came with them as their minister. They landed in Philadelphia September 8th. The brethren here treated them courteously, and advised them to settle in the vicinity of Pennypack, which they did, and continued there for two years. During that time they kept together as a distinct church, held meetings at each other's residences, and observed the ordinances of Christ. In the two years, twenty-one persons were added to their number. The ceremony of laying on of hands upon newly baptized converts prevailed among the Welsh churches at this period, and was observed by this emigrant church, but the Pennypack brethren disagreed, and for the sake of peace, the newly-settled body from Wales removed to Delaware, purchased a tract of land, and named the place "Welsh Tract." The church assumed the name, and to this day is known as "The Welsh Tract Baptist Church." Organized in Wales, and emigrating to this country as a church, it was called, for a long time, "The Emigrant Church."

Concerning the rite of laying on of hands, the Lower Dublin Church practiced it at the first, but, says Hon. H. G. Jones, "It afterwards grew indifferent on the subject. It was, however, continued in many churches, and at first the practice was insisted on as a term of Communion. Gradually, and after a free conference, the churches of Pennsylvania and Delaware agreed that the practice or disuse of the ordinance should not be a bar to Communion." In speaking of the Welsh Tract Church, Morgan Edwards says:—

It was the principal, if not sole, means of introducing singing, imposition of hands, church covenants, etc., among the Baptists in the Middle States. Singing psalms met with opposition, especially at Cohansey, but laying on of hands on baptized believers as such, gained acceptance with more difficulty, as appears from the following history translated from the Welsh Tract book, viz., "But we could not be in fellowship (at the Lord's table) with our brethren in Pennypack and Philadelphia, because they did not hold to the *laying on of hands*, and some other particulars relating to a church; true, some of them believed in the ordinance, but neither preached it nor practiced it; and when we moved to Welsh Tract, and left twenty-two of our members at Pennypack, and took some of their members down with us, the difficulty increased. We had many meetings to compromise matters, but to no purpose, till June 22d, 1706; then the following deputies (naming twenty-five persons) met at the house of Bro. Richard Miles, in Radnor, Delaware County, Pa., and agreed—

1. That a member of either church might transiently Commune with the other.
2. That a member who desired to come under the laying on of hands might have his liberty without offence.
3. That the votaries of the rite might preach or debate upon the subject with all freedom, consistent with charity and brotherly love.

But three years after this meeting we had reason to review the transaction, because of some brethren who arrived from Wales, and one among ourselves, who questioned whether the first article was warrantable; but we are satisfied that all was right, by the good effects which followed: for from that time forth our brethren held sweet communion together at the Lord's table, and our minister, Rev. Thomas Griffiths, was invited to preach and assist at an ordination at Pennypack, after the death of our Bro. Watts. He proceeded from thence to the Jerseys, where he enlightened many in the good ways of the Lord, insomuch that, in three years after, all the ministers and about twenty-five private members had submitted to the ordinance."

The above, from the Welsh Tract records, was translated by Morgan Edwards, and can be relied on. It affords proof that the practice of laying on of hands was nearly if not quite universal in all this section of the country.

On the 27th of August, 1702, Rev. John Watts, pastor of the Pennypack Church, died. He was buried in the graveyard adjoining the meeting-house. On his tombstone is the following acrostical inscription :—

> Interred here I be,
> Oh, that you could now see,
> How unto Jesus for to flee,
> Not in sin still to be.
> Warning in time pray take,
> And peace by Jesus make,
> Then at the last when you awake,
> Sure on his right hand you'll partake.

Mr. Watts was the first Baptist minister interred in Philadelphia. The sixteen years of his life spent here had been fraught with blessed results, in laying broad and deep in Bible truth, the foundations on which our denominational superstructure has since been rising with such magnificent proportions, to the glory of God and the praise of his grace.

The year of this pioneer's death was signalized by the disbanding of the church at Cold Spring, after an existence of eighteen years as the First Baptist Church in Pennsylvania. The members mostly united with the Pennypack organization, into the fellowship of which were baptized, during this year, thirteen persons, the largest number thus received, with one exception, during the first forty-four years of the church's history. For many years after the disbanding of the organization, there were members of Pennypack living at Cold Spring.

Ever since the act of clear-headed and simple justice, on the part of John Holme, Esq., relative to the dispute between the Keithian and Penn Quakers, there had been a friendly feeling among the former towards the Baptists, so that when the Baptists were unrighteously expelled from their original place of worship, and refused to go to law with their Christian brethren of another denomination to be reinstated in said house, the Keithians kindly offered them the use of their edifice. This was in 1707, when the Keithian "Society in a manner broke up," and together with the invited regular Baptists they became incorporated as one body.

The Keithian meeting-house, erected in 1692, was a small wooden building. It passed into the hands of the Baptists, and for nearly a quarter of a century was occupied by them. It stood on the identical spot in Lagrange Place, where for so many years the First Baptist Church maintained their edifice.

The meetings for conference sustained by the Lower Dublin Church developed the talents of their young men, and kept up a constant supply of preachers for their pulpit. These young men, too, were under the constant supervision and encouragement of the pastor, and acted as his assistants.

Upon the death of John Watts, the church called two of its members to ordination and the joint care of the congregation—Evan Morgan and Samuel Jones. The former was called to the ministry in 1702 and the latter in 1697. They were both ordained, October 23, 1706, by Rev. Thomas Killingsworth, of Cohansey, and Rev. Thomas Griffiths, of Welsh Tract. Rev. Evan Morgan's life in the active ministry was very short. He was born in Wales, and came to this country when young. He was originally a Quaker, but went off with the Keithians. He was baptized in 1697, by Thomas Rutter, at Southampton, in Bucks county, but the same year he renounced his connection with the Quakers and became a member at Lower Dublin. He was a man of marked piety, prudence and intelligence. Rev. Samuel Jones was born in Radnorshire, Wales, July 6, 1657, and was baptized there, in 1683, by Rev. Henry Gregory. He was a constituent member of the Lower Dublin Church, and gave the lot on which the meeting-house stands. The original house, built of stone, *twenty-five feet square*, was erected in 1707. The deed for the lot is dated Jan. 14, 1710.

The reader will make a distinction between the above Samuel Jones and the Rev. Dr. Samuel Jones, hereafter to be mentioned. Both have the same name, but it is the latter who became so celebrated in our denomination's work in this country.

The year 1707, made memorable by the erection, for the first time in Philadelphia, of a Baptist meeting-house, and, by the occupancy of another, which the First Church could call their own, was still further marked by the organization of the Philadelphia Baptist Association—the first, and, for over fifty years, the only Baptist Association in the country. This was on Saturday, July 27, 1707. As the Baptists commenced to worship in the Keithian meeting-house, March 15, 1707, it was in that unpretending frame structure this Association was organized. In the constituency of this Association it may be observed, the name of the Philadelphia Church does not appear. The reason was, that said body was regarded as a branch of the one at Lower Dublin, and the pastors of that church, for nearly fifty years, supplied the pulpit in Philadelphia. It is, nevertheless, a fact that in the meeting-house of the First Baptist Church, of this city, the Philadelphia Baptist Association started on its honored and successful career.

In his Century sermon,* Dr. Samuel Jones says:—

This association originated in what they called general, and sometimes yearly meetings. These meetings were instituted so early as 1688, and met alternately in May and September, at Lower Dublin, Philadelphia, Salem, Cohansie, Chester and Burlington; at which places there were members though no church or churches constituted, except Lower Dublin and Cohansie. At these meetings their labor was chiefly confined to the ministry of the word, and the administration of Gospel ordinances. But in the year 1707 they seem to have taken more properly the form of an Association; for then they had delegates from several churches, and attended to their general con-

---

* Century Minutes. page 454.

cerns. We, therefore, date our beginning as an association from that time; though we might, with but little impropriety, extend it back some years. They were at this time but a feeble band, though a band of faithful brothers, consisting of but five churches. The church at Lower Dublin, Piscataqua, Middletown, Cohansie and Welsh Tract.

In the Century Minutes* of the Association is the following account of the first meeting in 1707:—

There is no track or footsteps of any regular association, agreement, or confederation, between the first churches in these colonies of Pennsylvania and the Jerseys, that I can find, before the year 1707, when we have, in the records of the Church of Pennepeck, this account, viz.: Before our general meeting held at Philadelphia, in the seventh month, 1707, it was concluded by the several congregations of our judgment, to make choice of some particular brethren, such as they thought most capable in every congregation, and those to meet at the yearly meeting to consult about such things as were wanting in the churches, and to set them in order; and these brethren meeting at the said yearly meeting, which began the 27th of the seventh month, on the seventh day of the week, agreed to continue the meeting till the third day following in the work of the public ministry. It was then agreed that a person that is a stranger, that has neither a letter of recommendation, nor is known to be a person gifted, and of a good conversation, shall not be admitted to preach, nor be entertained as a member in any of the baptized congregations in communion with each other.

It was also concluded that if any difference shall happen between any member and the church he belongs unto, and they cannot agree, then the person grieved may, at the general meeting, appeal to the brethren of the several congregations, and with such as they shall nominate, to decide the difference; that the church and the person so grieved do fully acquiesce in their determination. It was also agreed That no man shall be allowed to preach among the Associated Churches, except he produce credentials of his being in communion with his church, and of his having been called and licensed to preach.

The object of this arrangement is thus stated by Morgan Edwards:—

Before this, vain and insufficient men who had set themselves up to be preachers, would stroll about the country under the name of Baptist Ministers; also, ministers degraded and ex-communicated, who, with their immorality too, brought disgrace on the very name of Baptist; which evil the above agreement of the Association, if attended

---

*Page 25.

to, would in a great measure remedy. Christ is the door to the ministry, and his church is the porter, for to it hath been given the keys; and whoever comes in at the door, to him the porter openeth, John x: 3; he that climbeth into the pulpit any other way, climbeth thither by an extraordinary call and mission, and must give an extraordinary proof thereof, as the Apostles did, or subject himself to a suspicion of intrusion and imposture. And it has been found, that they who pretend to extraordinary call and missions are such as could obtain no ordinary ones, because either their characters or gifts would not justify any church that should put them into the ministry. In truth they are self-made preachers; and it has been said that a "self-made preacher, a quack doctor, and a pettifogging lawyer, are three animals that the world would do better without than with."

Relative to the motive and object prompting to the organization of this Association, Hon. Horatio Gates Jones says:—

As the churches increased in number, and also in membership, various questions arose, both as to matters of faith and discipline. It was, of course, desirable for all the churches to have the same rules and to act in unity; and yet each Baptist church being independent of all others, it was apparent to the pastors and brethren that some general meeting was necessary where such questions could be freely and amicably discussed, and where counsel and advice could be given. Hence, it was proposed to *associate*, once a year, for this purpose, by representatives from the several churches. This annual meeting was, therefore, designated by the name of an "Association;" but it had no power or authority to bind the churches composing it, and from the very first was regarded as an *Advisory Council*—and such is the character of all Baptist Associations in America, as well as in all other parts of the world.

The vast field occupied by the church at Lower Dublin required an additional minister; so, on September 25th, 1708, Joseph Wood, a member of the church, was set apart by public ordination. He was born near Hull, in Yorkshire, England, in 1659, and came to America about 1684. He was baptized by Elias Keach, at Burlington, N. J., June 24th, 1691. He aided Revs. Evan Morgan and Samuel Jones, as co-pastor in their ministerial work. The following year two ministers, who had been prominently identified with our churches in this city, died—Rev. Thomas Killingsworth, of Cohansey, N. J., and Rev. Evan Morgan, of Pennypack. The latter passed away February 16th, 1709, and was buried near the church. Their loss was severely felt, but the Master raised up others to take their place. In 1810, three young men arrived from Wales—Jenkin Jones, Benjamin Griffith and David Davis, all of whom became ministers, and rendered successful service in the cause of God and truth, the effect of which is still felt in our Baptist Zion.

CHAPTER IV.—1711-1720.

DISSENSIONS.—RULING ELDERS.—THE FIFTH STREET GRAVEYARD.—
MONTGOMERY CHURCH ORGANIZED.—WM. THOMAS.—TUNKERS IN
GERMANTOWN.

FEBRUARY 14th, 1711, there was another welcome arrival on our shores—Rev. Abel Morgan. He was born in Wales in 1673. At the age of nineteen he began to preach the gospel, and in 1696 he was ordained. Highly esteemed by his church, it was a great trial to part with him for America. His voyage was a tedious and trying one. He was eleven weeks on the Atlantic Ocean, and twenty-two weeks in the vessel, as it was compelled to seek harbor twice before reaching its destination. On the journey his little boy died, and also his beloved wife. Their bodies were both committed to the deep. He was called to take the leading care of the church at Pennypack, which he accepted, and preached alternately there and in Philadelphia. He was a brother to Enoch Morgan, the third pastor of Welsh Tract, and a half brother to Benjamin Griffith, of Montgomery.

In the settlement of Philadelphia, there were persons of different nationalities and of every variety of temperament and opinion. It was not surprising, therefore, to find in church life, as we have already seen, much that was heterodox as well as much that was true. The church in Philadelphia was not to be exempt in this variety of opinion, as we learn from Morgan Edwards. He says :—

This church experienced a painful division in 1711, occasioned by the turbulent spirit of an Irish preacher, who was among them, along with Mr. Burrows. His name was Thomas Selby. When he had formed a party, he shut Mr. Burrows and his friends out of the meeting-house, who, henceforth, met at Mr. Burrows' house, in

DISSENSIONS.   49

Chestnut street. This was the situation of affairs when Mr. Abel Morgan arrived in 1711. But his presence soon healed the breach, and obliged Shelby to quit the town, which he did in 1713, and went to Carolina, and there he died, the same year, but not before he had occasioned much disturbance.

The Mr. Burrows referred to in the above was a Rev. John Burrows. He was a native of Taunton, in England, where he was ordained. In 1713 he became pastor of the Baptist Church of Middletown, New Jersey, where he maintained a successful ministry through a long life, and where he died in a good old age.

At the meeting of the Association in 1812, the disturbance caused by Thomas Selby was brought up and referred to a committee for adjustment, to which arrangement both parties consented. After a careful and thorough examination of all the facts, the committee reported as follows:—

With respect to the difference between the members and others, some time belonging to the Baptist church at Philadelphia, as it hath been laid before us, persons chosen by both sides, they having referred the whole of their difference to our determination; we, doing what in us lies for the glory of God, and the peace of the whole church, in regard of the transactions past, and what may be best for the future, for the interest of the gospel, upon due consideration of what hath been laid before us, as followeth, viz.: We do find the way and manner of dealing and proceeding with each other hath been from the rule of the gospel, and unbecoming Christians in many respects, and in some too shameful here to enumerate the particulars.

And first, we judge it expedient in point of justice, that Mr. Thomas Selby be paid the money subscribed to him by the members of this church, and be discharged from any further service in the work of the ministry; he being a person, in our judgment, not likely for the promotion of the gospel in these parts of the country; and, considering his miscarriages, we judge he may not be allowed to communion.

And secondly, as to the members of this congregation, we do apprehend the best way is, that each part offended do freely forgive each other all personal and other offences that may have arisen on this occasion, and that they be buried in oblivion; and that those who shall for future mention or stir up any of the former differences so as to tend to contention, shall be deemed disorderly persons, and be dealt with as such.

D

And thirdly, that those that exempted themselves from their communion on this account, except as above, be allowed to take their places orderly without contention, and such as refuse to be deemed disorderly persons.

Signed—Timothy Brooks, Thomas Shepherd, Thomas Abbott, John Drake, Nicolas Jonson, Dickason Shepherd, Job Shepherd, James Bollen, Samuel Jones, John Hart, John Bray.

Let it be noted, say the Century Minutes of the Association, that the said Thomas Selby, though he and his party referred as above said, yet he appeared afterwards very outrageous while he stayed in the province, and some of his adherents joined to other denominations, and never returned to seek their place in the church, and the church did accordingly exclude them. But the greatest part took their places personally.

From the year 1712 to the year 1720, though the churches maintained a yearly Association, yet there are no minutes of said meetings. Probably, during those years there was nothing of special importance brought before the Philadelphia Association. In the meantime several clergymen of our denomination, from different parts of Great Britain, were constantly arriving in Philadelphia. These located in New Jersey, Pennsylvania and Delaware, and did good service in the work of the Lord.

Among the early Baptist churches in this vicinity, for many years, was the office of *Ruling Elders*. The record book of the Pennypack Church, under date of June 19th, 1715, says: "A proposal was made for having Ruling Elders in the church; left to consideration till next Quarterly Meeting." That they had such officers down to 1763, is proven in the subsequent Minutes of the church.

In 1718, Richard Sparks, carpenter, who owned a lot of ground at the southeast corner of Market and Fifth streets, made the following devise of a lot for a burial ground for Seventh-Day Baptists:—

I do hereby devise one hundred feet of the back end of my lot on the south side of High street, in Philadelphia, for a burying place for the use of the people or society called the Seventh-Day Baptists, for-

FIFTH STREET GRAVE-YARD. 51

ever, in which said piece of ground I desire to be buried, my wife having the use of it during her natural life.

It is probable this one hundred feet, being on Fifth street, was used for burial purposes. There yet remains a very small part of this lot, which is walled in on Fifth street between the two wings of the Eastern Market House. Inside this enclosure, concealed from the street, is a marble tablet, with the following inscription:—

> This monument erected A. D. 1829, by the Trustees of the First Congregation of Seventh-Day Baptists, residing in the township of Hopewell, in the county of Cumberland, West New Jersey, and the Trustees of the Seventh-Day Baptist Church of Christ, in Piscataway, East New Jersey, to perpetuate the memory of Richard Sparks, who, in his testament and last will, gave and devised this lot for a burying ground for the use of the Society of Seventh-Day Baptists, and was himself interred therein, A. D. 1716, agreeably to his request in said will, with several other ancestors and relatives of members of the said societies, who were laid within twenty-five feet of the north end of the same.

A number of names follow this inscription, being those of the persons who erected the tablet.

The County of Montgomery, in Pennsylvania, was not formed until 1789; up to that time it was a part of Philadelphia County: the Montgomery Baptist Church, therefore, belongs to this history up to the separate organization of the county in which it is located. The first Baptist settlers in Montgomery were John Evans and Sarah his wife. They were members of a Baptist Church in Wales, and came here in 1710. The next year John James and Elizabeth his wife, from the same Principality, joined them. They were visited by Rev. Abel Morgan occasionally, who preached the word to all who came to hear, at the house of Mr. Evans. God's blessing attended these visits, and Mr. Morgan was permitted to baptize several persons. They were at length advised either to unite with the church at Pennypack, or else establish one in their own neighborhood. Not being familiar with the English language, and that church so distant, they concluded it was best they should organize one by themselves. Mr. Morgan approved this step, and on June 20th, 1719, they were constituted as a distinct Baptist

MONTGOMERY BAPTIST CHURCH.

Church, with nine or ten members. Revs. Abel Morgan and Samuel Jones were present to assist and direct in the work. The following is the interesting account of the proceedings as given in the Century Minutes of the Philadelphia Association*:—

The first part of the day was spent in fasting and prayer, with a sermon preached by Mr. Morgan, suitable to the occasion. Being asked whether they were desirous and freely willing to settle together as a church of Jesus Christ, they all answered in the affirmative; and being asked whether they were acquainted with one another's principles, and satisfied with one another's graces and conversation, it was also answered in the affirmative; and then for a demonstration of their giving themselves up, severally and jointly to the Lord, as a people of God and a church of Jesus Christ, they all lifted up their right

---

* Page 19.

hand. Then were they directed to take one another by the hand, in token of their union, declaring at the same time that as they had given themselves to God, so they did give themselves also to one another by the will of God, (2 Cor. viii. 5), to be a church according to the gospel; to worship God and to maintain the doctrines of the gospel, according to their ability, and to edify one another. Then were they pronounced and declared to be a church of Jesus Christ; a right hand of fellowship was given to them as a sister church, with exhortations and instructions suitable to the station and relation they now stood in; and the whole was finished with solemn prayer to God for a blessing on the work of the day.

Mr. Morgan visited them from time to time, and administered the ordinances among them. Elisha Thomas, of Welsh Tract, and other ministering brethren also preached to them as they had opportunity. All the early ministers of our denomination in this vicinity were eminently missionary in their character, hence, like the primitive disciples, they went everywhere preaching the word.

William Thomas and John James, members at Montgomery, by the constant exercise of their gifts, gave evidence of ability to preach the word, and were thus occupied frequently. The history of Mr. Thomas is of interest, and is thus given by the late Rev. Joseph Mathias, of Hilltown, whose praise is in all the older churches of this region:—

He arrived in this country about 1712, being entirely destitute of all worldly means, and in debt for all the expenses of the passage of himself and family; notwithstanding, when he left his native place, he was possessed of ample means to plant himself in circumstances of affluence in his new location. This calamity befell him in consequence of a most flagrant act of misconduct on the part of the commander of the vessel, in which his property was shipped, who sailed before the time set for him to come on board. He took passage on credit as early as possible, but on his arrival he had the mortification to find the captain had absconded, and all was lost; and to add to his grief and vexation, he identified his goods and clothes, etc., in the possession of new owners, which could never be recovered.

But being a man of energy, robust in person, and of great decision of character, he at once applied himself to industrious efforts, as many others in similar circumstances have done, and in process of time became a man of large possessions in lands in different places.

He built a meeting-house at his own expense, in which, for a number of years, he officiated in the ministry, and now, with many of his family, reposes in his own graveyard in Hilltown, where a suitable monument is erected to his memory.

I must record here the arrival in this city of another branch of the Baptist family. In the fall of the year 1719, about twenty families of the Tunkers, from Germany landed in Philadelphia, some of whom settled in Germantown. Morgan Edwards says of them, that they—

Are commonly called Tunkers, to distinguish them from the Mennonists, for both are styled Baptists. They are called Tunkers in derision, which is as much as "sops," from *tunken*, to put a morsel in sauce; but as the term signifies *dippers*, they may rest content with their nickname. They are also called *Tumblers*, from the manner in which they perform baptism, which is by putting the person head-forward under water (while kneeling), so as to resemble the motion of the body in the act of tumbling.

There being no minutes extant of the Philadelphia Association for this decade, save for one year, the materials for historical purposes are very meagre. Yet, from cotemporary history we are assured that the Baptists of this city were not unmindful of, nor disinterested in the important events transpiring about them. They rejoiced in the extension of Christ's kingdom in the regions beyond, in the organization, in 1715, of the first Baptist Church in Delaware county—at Brandywine. With others of this city, they mourned the death of William Penn, which took place at Rushcomb, England, July 30th, 1718. For the founder of Pennsylvania they ever had a profound regard, and to the last were among his loyal friends.

CHAPTER V.—1721-1730.

DEATH OF SAMUEL JONES AND ABEL MORGAN.—AN EDUCATED MINISTRY.—THOMAS HOLLIS.—HARVARD COLLEGE.—ORDER IN CHURCH SERVICES.—CAREFUL RECEPTION OF MINISTERS FROM ABROAD.—THE FOURTH COMMANDMENT.—MARRYING AN UNBELIEVER.—FORFEIT OF OFFICE AND MEMBERSHIP IN THE CHURCH.—LETTERS OF CHURCHES TO THE ASSOCIATION.—CLOSED DOORS.—TUNKER CHURCH ORGANIZED.—GEO. EAGLESFIELD.—BENJAMIN GRIFFITH ORDAINED.—RECEPTION OF MEMBERS FROM GREAT BRITAIN.—REV. JENKIN JONES AT PENNYPACK.—WILLIAM KINNERSLEY.—JOSEPH EATON ORDAINED.—CHURCH LETTERS NOT GRANTED.—LAYING ON OF HANDS IN ORDINATION.—FRATERNAL CORRESPONDENCE WITH LONDON.—THE FIRST CIRCULAR LETTER.

IN the year 1722 two of the pastors of the Pennypack Church died, Samuel Jones, on the 3d of February, and Abel Morgan, on the 16th of December. The first was interred at Pennypack and the latter in the graveyard adjoining the church in Philadelphia. In addition to the lot which Mr. Jones gave to the church, he also bequeathed to it for the use of the pastor several valuable books. Abel Morgan was a man of large influence, good judgment, and very firm in his adhesion to, and declaration of the doctrines of the Bible. He prepared a *Concordance of the Holy Scriptures* in the Welsh language, but did not live to see it published. It was, however, issued in 1730, with an Introduction by his brother, Enoch Morgan. He also prepared a *Confession of Faith* in Welsh, which was printed. In the fiftieth year of his age, after having faithfully preached Jesus for thirty years, the Lord called him home. His death was probably sudden, as in that year, at the meeting of the Association " it was proposed for the churches to make inquiry among themselves, if they have any young persons hopeful for the ministry and inclinable for learning; and if they have, to give notice of it to MR. ABEL MORGAN before the

1st of November, that he may recommend such to the Academy on Mr. Hollis, his account."

We know not but this is the first record among American Baptists looking to an educated Ministry. Mr. Thomas Hollis, here referred to, was a Baptist in London, England. He was a most liberal benefactor of Harvard College, in Cambridge, near Boston. In that institution he founded two professorships, one of Divinity and the other of Mathematics. He also presented a valuable apparatus for mathematical and philosophical experiments, and at different times augmented the library with many valuable books. In 1727, the net production of his donation, exclusive of gifts not vendible, amounted to four thousand nine hundred pounds, the interest of which he directed to be appropriated to the support of the two professors, to the Treasurer of the College, and to ten poor students in divinity of suitable qualifications. It might be an interesting question for American Baptists to ask the Corporation of Harvard College what has become of this money.

At the time of the death of Samuel Jones and Abel Morgan, both of whom participated in the services connected with the constitution of the Montgomery Church, that body had so increased in number and in gifts that they called John James, David Evans, Benjamin Griffith and Joseph Eaton to exercise their talents with a view to the ministry. All of these were born in Wales.

The churches of that day were very desirous that the services of the Lord's house should be conducted with proper decorum, and very careful respecting the admission to their churches and their pulpits of men from abroad. This was illustrated at the Association convened Sept. 23, 1723, by an agreement then made, and by a query from the church at Brandywine, as to how "they might improve their vacant days of worship, when they have no minister among them to carry on the public work?"

Solution.—We conceive it expedient that the church do meet together as often as conveniency will admit; and when they have none to carry on the work of preaching, that they read a chapter, sing a psalm, and go to prayer and beg of God to increase their grace and comfort, and have due regard to order and decency in the exercise of those gifted at all times, and not to suffer any to exercise their gifts in a mixed multitude until tried and approved of first by the church.

Agreed that the proposal drawn by the several ministers, and signed by many others, in reference to the examination of all gifted brethren and ministers that come in here from other places, be duly put in practice, we having found the evil of neglecting a true and previous scrutiny in those affairs.

At the next meeting of this body, in 1724, it was queried "concerning the fourth commandment, whether changed, altered or diminished?" The Association answered by referring to the article on the Sabbath, in the Confession of Faith as set forth by the messengers met in London, in 1679. That article is very plain and decided relative to the strict observance of the Lord's day in the worship of God.

It was further asked at the same meeting, "Whether a believer may marry an unbeliever, without coming under church censure for it?" and was answered in the negative. A query was also presented, "Whether an officer in the church who forfeits his office, forfeits his membership?" Answered in the negative. But if he forfeits his membership, he forfeits his office. Whether he, if restored to his membership, must also be restored to office, is another case not here considered.

The propriety of this answer is apparent. If a minister or a deacon be excluded from a church, the exclusion necessarily carries with it deposition from the ministry and from the deaconship. There can be no recognized official standing in the ministry, when there is none in the church.

It was further "concluded and agreed," in connection

with the above query and answer, "That a church ought to be unanimous in giving their voice in choosing and setting up, or deposing one set up, to act in any church office, or to act as an officer in the church. Any act of that nature, commenced without common consent, is void, and hath no power in it."

At this session of the Association we have the first reference to letters from the churches, and the authority for the character of their contents, and, perhaps, for the length they have since attained in some quarters. It was then

Concluded that the letters from the churches to the Association, hereafter, may contain salutations, comtemplations, congratulations, etc., in one page, and the complaints, queries or grievances, etc., be written apart; for it is agreed that the former shall be read publicly the first day of the Association's meeting, and the latter, the church's doubts, fears or disorders, etc., be opened and read to the Association only.

It is evident from the last part of the above that the Philadelphia Baptist Association transacted some of their business, in those days, with closed doors.

By Dec. 25, 1723, the Tunkers had so increased in Germantown that on that day they organized themselves into a church, which is still extant and vigorous.

As already stated, the church in Philadelphia had no settled minister among them; being regarded as a branch of Pennypack, the pastors of the latter supplied them with preaching. "They did, indeed," says Mr. Edwards, "in 1723, choose George Eaglesfield to preach to them, contrary to the sense of the church at Pennypack; but in 1725 he left them and went to Middletown," and preached to the church there until his death.

Benjamin Griffith was ordained to the gospel ministry, Oct. 23, 1725, and became the first pastor of the church at Montgomery, of which, for several years, he had been an exemplary and earnest member. Revs. Elisha Thomas and

Jenkin Jones assisted in the services of ordination. In view of a recent claim in Wales, that the above is an ancestor of the Rev. Benjamin Griffith, D. D., at present the honored and successful Secretary of the American Baptist Publication Society, we deem it proper to state that the claim is without foundation.

This church was soon called to receive members who had been dismissed under peculiar circumstances, as the following query from them to the Association, in 1726, intimates:—

In case there might be a division, and on the division a rent and separation follow in any church in Great Britain, and each party combining together in church form, each being sound in the faith, and during the separation both parties recommend members unto us here, as in full communion with them, how may the churches here proceed in such a case?

Answer.—We do advise that the churches here may take no further notice of the letters by such persons brought here, than to satisfy themselves that such are baptized persons, and of a regular conversation, and to take such into church covenant as if they had not been members of any church before.

We come now to the settlement of Rev. Jenkin Jones in the pastorate of the Pennypack Church, which occurred June 17, 1726. He was born in Wales in 1696, and came to this country in 1710. He does not seem to have been a member of a church when he left Wales. He was called to the ministry in Welsh Tract in 1724, and removed to Philadelphia in 1725.

William Kinnersley was an assistant to Mr. Jones, at Pennypack, in connection with Rev. Joseph Wood, already mentioned. Mr. Kinnersley was born in Leominster, England, in 1669. He came to America Sept. 12, 1714, and was never ordained. Oct. 24, 1727, Joseph Eaton was ordained to the gospel ministry at Montgomery, and became the assistant to the pastor, Benjamin Griffith, who, with Rev. Elisha Thomas, participated in the ordination services.

This church presented a practical query to the Association, in 1728, "Whether a church is bound to grant a letter of dismission to any member to go to another church, while his residence is not removed?" Answered in the negative, "we having neither precept nor precedent for such a practice in Scripture."

How the subject of laying on of hands was regarded at this time may be learned from a query presented by the branch church at Philadelphia, to the Association, in 1729, "Suppose a gifted brother, who is esteemed an orderly minister by or among those that are against the laying on of hands in any respect, should happen to come amongst our church, whether we may allow such an one to administer the ordinance of baptism and the Lord's Supper, or no?" Answered in the negative; "because it is contrary to the rule of God's word; see Acts xiii: 2, 3, and xiv: 23, compared with Titus i: 5, and Tim. iv: 14, from which prescribed rules we dare not swerve." This year arrangements were made for opening up a fraternal correspondence between the Association and prominent Baptists in London.

It was customary on the part of the Association to send back to the churches a short circular letter containing a general statement of the meeting that had been held, and urging to faithfulness to Christ, to the church, and in developing any special matter of great importance. The first of these we have given us was in 1729. It is as follows:—

The elders and messengers of the baptized congregations in Pennsylvania and the Jerseys, met at Philadelphia, Sept. 27th and 28th, 1729, in a solemn Association, sendeth greeting:

Dearly beloved brethren in the Lord Jesus Christ: We heartily rejoice to see your care, diligence, requests and desires, on our own behalf, at the throne of grace; and also your care and diligence in maintaining our yearly correspondence and communion in the gospel. We, your representatives met together in love, perused your letters and gladly received your messengers. We find cause to rejoice that God has crowned the labors of his ministers with such success. There have been considerable additions the past year, in several churches, and some in most. Praise be rendered to our gracious God, we find the churches generally to be at peace and unity among themselves. We think it expedient to give you an account of our proceedings. We conferred together, without any jars or contentions in our debates; our souls have been refreshed, hearing of the welfare of the churches in general; also in hearing the sweet and comfortable truths of the gospel declared among us by the faithful labors of our ministering brethren, which we hope is to the glory of God and the good of souls. We earnestly desire you to walk worthy of your holy vocation, standing fast and striving together for the faith of the gospel. It is the general complaint of many that there is much lukewarmness and deadness in matters of religion, which we hope is not a mere compliment, but rather the grief of the churches. In order to remedy this soul distemper, our advice and desire is that you be diligent to keep your places in the house of God; be frequent and instant in prayer, both in secret and in public; strive after the life and power of religion; make religion your earnest business; keep your garments undefiled from the world; walk as becomes saints before God and men; improve your opportunities in all religious duties, both among your families and in the church. Stand fast for the defending and maintaining of the ordinances of Christ; wait on God in them, that you may reap the benefits of Christ by them. Strive to keep together, maintaining the unity of the Spirit in the bond of peace; always resisting the assaults of Satan, who waiteth opportunities to disturb the peace of God's children. Be careful that you do nothing that may tend to breed disturbances in the church of God.

From this excellent epistle, the first of the kind extant in this country, has sprung the various styles of circular letters now furnished in our different Associational meetings. All those of the Philadelphia Association would, if gathered together, furnish a valuable, interesting and profitable book. In 1729, for the first time, the names of the messengers (twenty-two in all) to the Association appear. They are as follows:—

Jno. David, Ben Stelle, Owen Thomas, Geo. Hugh, Gershom Mott, Joseph Eaton, Jno. Devonald, John Welledge, Wm. Kinnersley, Samuel Osgood, John Clarkson, John Holmes, Jeremiah Kollet, John Bartholomew, John Heart, Robert Chalfant, Elisha Thomas, George Eaton, Dickison Shephard, Jenkin Jones, Ebenezer Smith, Simon Butler.

A century and a half has passed away since these names were registered. Most of them are now strange in our Baptist Zion, but others are yet quite familiar. Descendants of these honored men are still identified with God's Israel, and worthily working for that cause so dear to the fathers.

CHAPTER VI.—1731-1740.

FIRST BAPTIST MEETING-HOUSE BUILT.—ASSISTANCE NEEDED.—BAPTISTS AND THE ROMANISTS.—CHURCH OF ENGLAND DEMANDS THE BAPTIST PROPERTY.—FAIL TO GET IT.—WILLIAM KINNERSLEY DIES. —SAMUEL JONES AND SAMUEL STILLMAN.—REV. GEORGE WHITEFIELD ARRIVES.—A SPIRITUAL MAN.—REV. JENKIN JONES.—VARIOUS QUESTIONS.—ASSOCIATION RECORDS.—CATECHETICAL INSTRUCTION.—FIFTY-SIX BAPTIZED.—DENOMINATIONAL GROWTH SLOW.

WITH the constant growth of Philadelphia, and the corresponding progress of the Baptist congregation, a larger and more attractive meeting-house was needed, hence the old frame structure, which had stood for nearly forty years, was taken down, and in 1731, on the same spot, a neat *brick building* was erected. This was 42 by 30 feet. To build this edifice was a great burden upon them, as they informed the Association that year " that they have been at a great charge in building a meetinghouse, which is to be very heavy, unless the rest of the churches of the same order will find it in their hearts to contribute towards the defraying of the same."

The scrupulous regard of Baptists for the rights of conscience and religious liberty were exerting a good influence. The position taken by John Holme, the Baptist magistrate, in 1692, relative to religious disputes, had not been forgotten, and the members of the denomination maintained that all, of every creed, should freely maintain their religious belief, and enjoy that liberty which was guaranteed to them by the Charter of Pennsylvania. This was their position in 1733, when a few families of the Roman Catholic faith, had arrived and erected a small chapel in Philadelphia. The colonial officers were alarmed at this movement, and Governor Gordon brought the matter before the Council, and informed them that "a house had been lately built on Walnut street, in Philadelphia, wherein mass was openly celebrated by a Catholic priest, contrary to the laws of England." The citizens of the Baptist persuasion and others claimed that Catholics and all other sects were protected by the laws which had been established by William Penn, and that all were equally entitled to religious liberty. The Council, therefore, wisely refrained from any interference.

In January, 1731, the Assembly of Pennsylvania had a bill before it, enabling religious societies to purchase lands for churches, meeting-houses and the like. The members of Christ Church took exception to this bill as it would injure the right which they considered certain of their number possessed in the lot on which the Baptist meeting-house stood. But the bill passed. The Christ Church people then tried to induce the Governor to withhold his signature from the bill. This opposition was really aroused because the Baptists, who had held their property for twenty-six years, still claimed it. The Keithians had conveyed the lot to Thomas Budd, Thomas Peart, Ralph Ward and James Poulter, in fee, to hold it for the Christian Quakers, for a meeting-house, and for such use or uses as the major part of them should appoint, allow or approve of. It was *averred* by the Episcopalians that a majority of the Keithians became members of Christ Church, particularly Thomas Peart and Ralph Ward, and that they had been granted the use of the Keithian meeting-house. The Baptists replied that they had occupied the property by invitation of the Keithians for twenty-six years, and that the Keithians had become Baptists. As to the occupancy of the property by Christ Church, the Baptists said,

> Before the Church of England had any public place of worship, the Society (Keithians or Christian Quakers) did, at their request, grant to the said church the use of the house and lot, now in contro-

versy, between the hours of twelve and three, on each Sunday, the said Society themselves assembling there at other hours, both before and after, in the same day. This permission graciously given could not by any ingenuity be tortured into a conveyance of the title to the property.

In 1733, Thomas Peart, the only surviving trustee, deeded the property to Christ Church for charitable purposes.

"In 1734," says Mr. Edwards, "an incident occurred that like to have deprived the church both of their house and lot; for then one Thomas Peart died, after having made a conveyance of the premises to the Church of England. The vestry demanded possession, but the Baptists refused, and a lawsuit commenced, which brought the matter to a hearing before the Assembly. The Episcopalians being discouraged offered to give up the claim for £50. The offer was accepted and contention ceased."

On the 13th of February, 1734, William Kinnersley, an assistant minister at Pennypack, died. He was the father of Rev. Ebenezer Kinnersley, hereafter to be mentioned.

In the year 1737 there arrived in this city, with his parents, a little boy only two years of age. His name was Samuel Jones. Probably no one was then impressed with the possibilities that were wrapt up in the future of that lad, as, for the first time, he placed his feet on the wharf at Philadelphia. But, before his death, at Lower Dublin, in 1814, he rose to distinction and great usefulness, as will be seen. In the same year another Samuel appeared in this city, who was destined to equal renown. He was born here on the 27th of February, spent the early part of his life here, and in this, his native city, was married to a Miss Morgan. Entering the ministry, he frequently visited Philadelphia, but the scene of his greatest efficiency was in Boston. I refer to Rev. Samuel Stillman, D. D.

On Saturday, November 2d, 1739, Rev. George Whitefield arrived in Philadelphia. In his diary for the following

Monday is this record: "Was visited in the afternoon by the *Presbyterian* minister. Went afterwards to see the Baptist minister, who seems to be a spiritual man." The next day both of these ministers visited Whitefield. Rev. Jenkin Jones was the Baptist minister referred to, and the reference of the renowned and godly Whitefield to the spirituality of the man is a worthy compliment to one of the ablest and most useful of the early Baptists of this city.

A variety of questions were each year presented to the Association, some of them very practical and others, at this day, seem without point, yet when presented were doubtless regarded as important. By the year 1735, many in the Association awoke to the importance of keeping a regular record of the proceedings of that body. An effort was made to secure a minute book, and to elect a clerk and an assistant, but the matter failed. There were those then, as now, who could not see the importance of keeping such a record.

Realizing the necessity of catechetical instruction, the Association, in 1738,

Agreed, that since the catechisms are expended, and a few or none to be had, and our youth thereby not likely to be instructed in the fundaments of saving knowledge, that the several congregations we represent should consult amongst themselves what they can raise of money for so good a design, and send, against the 1st of May next, by their letters, to Mr. Jenkin Jones or John Holme, in Philadelphia, that they may know what number to draw out of press.

The entire number of persons baptized in this city, during this decade, in connection with the Baptist churches, was only fifty-six. The town was comparatively small, the people very much scattered, and the growth of the denomination slow, yet in that very slowness enterprises were inaugurated, principles maintained and beginnings made, which have contributed towards the subsequent permanence and growth of the churches here and elsewhere.

CHAPTER VII.—1741-1750.

PHILADELPHIA CONFESSION OF FAITH.—SUBSEQUENT EDITIONS.—SUBJECTS OF ARTICLES.—EBENEZER KINNERSLEY ORDAINED.—DOUBTS ON WHITEFIELD'S PREACHING.—ELECTRICITY.—JOSEPH EATON'S DEFECTION.—FIRST BAPTIST CHURCH RECONSTITUTED.—GROUNDLESS QUESTION.—CONSTITUENT MEMBERS.—THE SOUTHAMPTON BAPTIST CHURCH.—GEORGE EATON AND PETER P. VANHORN.— ABRAHAM LEVERING.—FIRST RECORDS OF THE ASSOCIATION.— BENJAMIN GRIFFITH.—POWER AND DUTY OF AN ASSOCIATION.— DEATH OF REV. JOSEPH WOOD—TROUBLE WITH THE PENNYPACK PROPERTY.—DEATH OF REV. JOSEPH EATON.—REV. ISAAC EATON AND HOPEWELL ACADEMY.—MODERATOR'S NAME FIRST GIVEN.— NATHANIEL JENKINS.

IN 1742 the Philadelphia Baptist Association adopted the Confession of Faith, set forth by the messengers of baptized congregations, met in London in 1689; a short treatise on Church Discipline; an article concerning the singing of psalms in the worship of God, and one relative to the laying on of hands upon baptized believers. These were printed in one volume by Benjamin Franklin, in 1743. A few copies of this issue are still extant, but they are in the hands of private parties. Subsequent editions were issued in 1773, 1798 and 1831.

The subjects of the various articles in the Confession of Faith, as published in 1742, are in the following order :— Holy Scriptures; God and the Holy Trinity; God's Decrees; Divine Providence; Fall of Man; Sin and Punishment Thereof; God's Covenant; Christ the Mediator; Free Will; Effectual Calling; Justification; Adoption; Sanctification; Saving Faith; Repentance Unto Life and Salvation; Good Works; Perseverance of the Saints; Assurance of Grace and Salvation; the Law of God; the Gospel and the Extent of the Grace Thereof; Christian Liberty and Liberty of Conscience; Religious Worship and the Sabbath-day; Singing of Psalms in Public Worship; Lawful Oaths and Vows; the Civil Magistrate; Marriage; the Church; the Communion of Saints; Baptism and the Lord's Supper; Baptism; Laying on of Hands; State of Man After Death, and the Resurrection of the Dead; the Last Judgment. In all thirty-four articles.

The treatise on Church Discipline has articles on—a True and Orderly Church; Ministers, &c.; Ruling Elders; Deacons; Admission of Church Members; Duties of Church Members; the Manifold Duties of Christians, especially to the Household of Faith; Church Censures—Admonition—Suspension—Excommunication.

In 1743, Ebenezer Kinnersley was ordained to the work of the gospel ministry. He was born in Gloucester, England, November 30, 1711. In 1714 his father removed to America and settled near the Pennypack Church. On the 6th of September, 1735, young Kinnersley was baptized and became a member of that church. Hon. Horatio Gates Jones, in his History of Lower Dublin Baptist Church, says of him:—

> Owing to delicate health and other objects of interest that engaged his attention, he never became a pastor. He was one of the few, in Philadelphia, who had doubts in regard to the character of the preaching which was introduced by Whitefield; nor did he hesitate to enter a solemn protest against it from the pulpit of the Baptist church. This happened on the 6th of July, 1740, and the excitement produced by the sermon was so great that he was absolutely forbidden the privilege of the Communion. For some time he attended the Episcopal church, but ere long the difficulty was settled, and when the Philadelphia Church was organized as a distinct society from that at Pennypack, he was one of the constituent members, and remained connected with it to his death. The year 1746 marked an epoch in his life; for his attention was then first directed to the wonderful and unknown properties of the *Electric Fire*, as it was then termed.

He became an intimate companion of Benjamin Franklin, and one of the most remarkable scientists of his day.

JOSEPH EATON'S DEFECTION.

In the year 1744 a difficulty occurred at Montgomery. Rev. Joseph Eaton rejected the literal sense of the eternal generation and sonship of Jesus Christ. The brethren of the ministry labored with him in a Christian spirit, and at the meeting of the Association he dismissed his skepticism on the subject, so that what threatened to be a serious matter was speedily healed, and this great and all-important doctrine not only firmly believed in but also faithfully promulgated.

The year which witnessed Kinnersley's attention first directed to the properties of electricity was signalized by the distinct organization of the First Baptist Church. Having been regarded as a branch of Pennypack, a question arose whether said church was not entitled to a part of the legacies bestowed on the branch in Philadelphia. This was a groundless question, but for fear the design of their benefactors should be perverted, the church, then consisting of fifty-six members, was formally constituted May 15, 1746. Letters of dismission for this purpose had been granted by Pennypack on the 3d of May. Having had, and exercised in reality, all the functions of a church from the first establishment in 1698, that year is certainly the proper one to date the commencement of their history. Rev. Jenkin Jones now severed his connection as pastor of the mother church and became the first pastor of the one in Philadelphia.

The account of the above transaction is given in the records of the parent church, as follows:—

April 5, 1746; the members of the church at Pennypack, residing at the city of Philadelphia, petitioned to the monthly meeting at Pennypack for a separation for themselves and for Mr. Jenkin Jones, the pastor of the church, also (his residence being among them), to answer which the church at Pennypack took a month to consider.

May 3, 1746; the church at Pennypack having considered their brethren's reasons for a separation, and finding them to be of weight, a dismission was granted, and they were soon after constituted and settled a regular gospel church, and their messengers were received at the next annual Association at Philadelphia.

The names of the constituent members were: JENKIN JONES, EBENEZER KINNERSLEY, William Branson, Andrew Edge, Thomas Pearse, Stephen Anthony, Augustus Stillman, Samuel Ashmead, Matthias Ingles, John Perkins, John Standeland, Robert Shewell, John Biddle, Joseph Crean, Henry Hartley, John Lewis, Joseph Ingles, Samuel Burkilo, John Catla, Thomas Byles, John Bazely, Samuel Morgan, Lewis Rees, Mary Standeland, Hannah Farmer, Mary Catla, Ann Yerkes, Mary Burkilo, Mary Prig, Hannah Crean, Ann Davis, Hannah Bazely, Jane Giffin, Edith Bazely, Uslaw Lewis, Jane Loxley, Esther Ashmead, Hannah Jones, Sarah Branson, Catherine Anthony, Jane Pearse, Mary Edge, Mary Valecot, Elizabeth Shewell, Mary Middleton, Frances Holwell, Elizabeth Sallows, Mary Morgan, Ann Hall, Phebe Hartley, Ann White.

SOUTHAMPTON BAPTIST CHURCH.

As already intimated, the pastors of the Pennypack church were accustomed to preach in all the region round about, and one of their stations was at Southampton, in Bucks county. Here the favor of God had been so manifest that, in three days after the dismission to reconstitute the church in Philadelphia, forty-eight members, all from Pennypack, were organized, April 8, 1746, into the Southampton Baptist Church. Religious services had been held there for many years, for John Morris, a member of Pennypack, who died February 22, 1733, aged 83 years, gave the ground for the meeting-house at Southampton and a farm of one hundred and twenty-five acres for the minister's use. This church was at once received into the Philadelphia Association and remained connected with that body for eighty-eight years. Those eminent ministers, Isaac Eaton and Oliver Hart, were originally members of this church. The removal of these one hundred and four members from Pennypack to constitute the two churches named, diminished the number who remained very considerably.

They at once took measures, however, to be supplied with preaching. George Eaton and Peter Peterson Vanhorn had already been called to exercise their gifts. A vote was taken by ballot, relative to their ordination, beginning with the former, as he was the elder, but he was not chosen, greatly to his mortification. The matter was then deferred, and Rev. Jenkin Jones continued to visit them once a month and administer the ordinances. At the request of Mr. Eaton another vote on his case was taken April 16, 1747. This time it was by rising and not by ballot. He was again rejected, but on the same day Mr. Vanhorn was elected, and he was ordained to the work of the ministry among them June 18, 1747. Revs. Jenkin Jones, Benjamin Griffith, John Davis and Joshua Potts participated in the services. Mr. Vanhorn was born at Middletown, in Bucks county, August 24th, 1719, and assumed the pastoral care of Pennypack October 31, 1747. It is possible that Mr. Vanhorn extended his labors, occasionally, over to Roxborough, twelve miles westward of his own church, as on May 16,

1751, he officiated at the marriage of William Levering of that place. Mr. Levering was a brother of Abraham Levering, who became a constituent member of the Roxborough Church, and its first deacon. In 1754 it is known that Mr. Vanhorn preached in Roxborough.

Thirty-nine years of the Association's history had now passed away, yet there had been no attempt to keep regular records of its doings, nor had any history of the denomination in this vicinity been written. Awaking to the importance of such records, the Association, in 1746, "Concluded, that Brother Benjamin Griffith should collect and set in order the accounts of the several Baptist churches in these provinces; and that the several churches should draw out and send him, as soon as possible, what accounts they have on record in church books of their respective constitutions, and by whose ministry they have been supplied." He performed this duty faithfully, and the work begun by him, when the Minutes of the Association were not printed, is preserved in a large folio volume, the greater part of which forms the first eighty pages of the Century Minutes of the Association. But for his valuable labors in this direction the early history of the Association might not now be obtained. In 1749 he prepared and read an essay on "The Power and Duty of an Association," which the Association directed to be recorded in their folio volume.

September 15, 1747, Rev. Joseph Wood, the fifth pastor at Pennypack, passed away from earth, at the advanced age of eighty-eight years. He was buried at Cold Spring, Bucks county. No vestige of his grave now remains, but in the resurrection those who sleep in Jesus will God bring with him.

The year after his death this church had considerable trouble about its property. It had been deeded to certain trustees, all of whom were dead, except George Eaton, who did not feel very kindly to the church, because it had not called him to ordination as a gospel minister. He, therefore, secretly deeded the property to other trustees who were friendly to him. This was discovered, and after considerable trouble and careful management the matter was rectified. The year following, 1749, Rev. Joseph Eaton, formerly of Montgomery, died. He was a brother of the above named George Eaton, and was only a little boy of seven years when he arrived, in 1686, in this country with his father, John Eaton. God raised him up to do much good. He was the father of Rev. Isaac Eaton, A. M., who was the first pastor of the church in Hopewell, New Jersey, and the first man in this country among the Baptists who established an academy for the purpose of promoting ministerial education. In his church, it is supposed, partially originated the plan for the formation of Brown University, in Rhode Island. He was its early friend, and Manning, Smith and others of his pupils were among the first to move in its establishment.

In 1749 we learn for the first time the name of the Moderator of the Philadelphia Association. It was Nathaniel Jenkins, a name worthy to stand at the head of as noble a list of excellent Christian men as ever graced a similar position in any religious organization.

CHAPTER VIII.—1751-1760.

FEEBLE CHURCHES SUPPLIED WITH PREACHING.—MINISTERS ORDAINED AT THE ASSOCIATION.—OTHER ASSOCIATIONS ORGANIZED.—GEORGE EATON CALLED TO THE MINISTRY.—EBENEZER KINNERSLEY, A PROFESSOR IN THE UNIVERSITY OF PENNSYLVANIA.—NEW BRITAIN CHURCH CONSTITUTED—JOHN DAVIS ORDAINED.—THE PIONEER BAPTISTS OF MARYLAND.—ORDINATION CERTIFICATE.—FIRST LATIN GRAMMAR SCHOOL.—HOPEWELL ACADEMY.—ASSOCIATION'S JUBILEE.—TALENTS DEVELOPED.—MINISTERIAL SUPPLY.—DOCTRINAL SERMON.—MEAGRE RECORDS.—FIRST CHURCH PULPIT SUPPLIED.—APPLICATION TO ENGLAND FOR A PASTOR - DEATH OF REV. JENKIN JONES.—HIS LEGACY.—DISSENTING MINISTERS PERMITTED TO SOLEMNIZE MARRIAGES.—MOUNT MORIAH CEMETERY.—REV. MORGAN EDWARDS INVITED FROM ENGLAND.—FIRST FRUIT OF THE HOPEWELL SCHOOL.—REV. JOHN GANO.—REV. SAMUEL STILLMAN.—VARIOUS OCCURRENCES.

IN the early days of the Philadelphia Association, much attention was paid to fostering the feeble churches connected with it. The strong supported the weak, and the ministers were appointed to visit, preach to, and counsel with the smaller bands. The ordination of brethren to the ministry was frequently under the supervision of the Association, and it was not an uncommon event to have a brother publicly set apart to the work of preaching the gospel during the meetings of the Association. Up to this decade the Philadelphia had been the only Baptist Association in the country, but with the growth of the Colonies and the spread of Baptist principles, the number of churches multiplied, and steps were taken to organize such bodies in different parts of the country, beginning with Charleston, South Carolina, in 1751.

By February 25th, 1752, the difficulties between the church at Pennypack and George Eaton were so far settled, he having shown a better Christian spirit and more fitness for the work, that the church on that day called him to exercise his gifts in the ministry "once a month and at burials."

In 1753, Rev. Ebenezer Kinnersley was elected Principal of the English school connected with the College of this city. This position he held until July 11th, 1755, when he was elected Professor of Rhetoric in the College. Such were his eminent abilities that in 1757, the Trustees of the Institution conferred upon him the degree of Master of Arts—a degree then as valuable as it was rare.

In 1754, the differences of opinion at Montgomery resulted in a separation, which led to the constitution of the church at New Britain, thus furnishing religious advantages to the people located in that vicinity. In 1756, John Davis was ordained to the work of the ministry at Montgomery. He was born at Pennypack, September 10th, 1721. After his ordination, he removed to Maryland and was the great pioneer of our denomination in that state. Relative to him in the Minutes of the Association for 1758, we find the following Testimonial:—

Ordered that a testimonial be given and signed by the Rev. Jenkin Jones, minister of the Baptist meeting or congregation in Philadelphia, to the Rev. John Davis, late of Bucks County, in Pennsylvania, but now of Baltimore county, in the province of Maryland, certifying his regular ordination, according to the rites, ceremonies and approved forms and usages of the Baptist church, and also his purity of life, manners and conversation; and recommending him to the favor of all Christian people, where he now does, or may hereafter dwell.

In pursuance of the above order, the following was given:—

To all Christian people to whom these presents shall come, I, Jenkin Jones, minister of the Baptist meeting or congregation of the city of Philadelphia, do send and certify, that the bearer hereof, Mr. John Davis, late of Bucks county, in the province of Pennsylvania, but now residing and dwelling in Baltimore county, in the province of Maryland, in the month of April, in the year of our Lord, one thousand seven hundred and fifty-six, was regularly admitted, ordained and received holy order to preach the gospel of our Lord and Saviour Jesus Christ, to all the people, according to the rites and ceremonies and approved forms and usages of the Baptist church; and that at all times, before and since his ordination aforesaid, for anything heard, known or believed to the contrary, he lived a holy and unblemished life, as well in his conversation as in his actions. And I do humbly recommend him to the notice, esteem and regard of all Christians where he now does or hereafter may reside, or with whom he may have conversation or dealing.

In testimony whereof and by order of the general meeting or Association aforesaid, I have hereunto set my hand, at the city of Philadelphia, the sixth day of October, in the year of our Lord, one thousand seven hundred and fifty-eight. JENKIN JONES.

The above document illustrates the character of ordination certificates, as well as the care taken in drawing them up, and in furnishing the ordained with them, more than a hundred years ago.

The churches were becoming impressed with the importance of providing means and encouraging institutions for furnishing a liberal education to the young, and especially to those who were to enter the ministry. Hence, at the Association in 1756, it was "Concluded to raise a sum

HOPEWELL ACADEMY, HOPEWELL, NEW JERSEY.

of money towards the encouragement of a Latin Grammar School for the promotion of learning amongst us, under the care of Brother Isaac Eaton, and the inspection of our brethren, Abel Morgan, Isaac Stille, Abel Griffith and Peter Peterson Vanhorn."

This was the first effort in this vicinity to raise money for educational purposes under the auspices of our denomination. The beginning was small, very insignificant, but from it has grown that magnificent system of, and facility for education among us in which we feel such a pride and interest. The following year the Association again "concluded to request the churches to contribute their mite towards the support of the Latin Grammar School, to promote useful learning among us." In 1758 it was again " Resolved, to desire our churches to continue a contribution toward a Grammar School, under consideration that what has been done hitherto in that way appears to have been well laid out, there being a number of well inclined youths applying themselves to learning therein."

In 1757, the Association had been in existence fifty years, and by that time twenty-five churches, situated respectively in the provinces of Pennsylvania, New Jersey, Delaware, Connecticut, New York, Virginia and Maryland had become connected with it.

The dismissal of members from Montgomery to constitute the church at New Britain, led to the more earnest development, as is often the case, of the talent that remained. Accordingly several young brethren gave evidence of ability to preach the Word; hence, at the Association in 1757, "In answer to a request from Kingwood, New Jersey, for ministerial supply, we advise them to apply to Montgomery, principally, and to others, as occasion requires." It was decided further, at the same session, " In consideration of the very great necessity for ministerial labor in many of the churches belonging to this Association, we request the church of Montgomery to send some of her young ministers to supply them as often as possible."

It 1759, it was decided that the opening sermon before the Association should be " upon one of the fundamental articles of the Christian faith," the subject to be assigned the year before. Hence, for a number of years, a Doctrinal sermon was delivered on some one or other of the articles of faith as adopted by the Association.

The Records of the First Baptist Church during the first fourteen years of its separate history are very meagre. For the first eleven years there are none at all. There was no attempt to keep a minute of the proceedings until August 11, 1760. A few fragments of minutes are found in the first Book of Records commencing with February 4, 1757. From these we learn that Rev. Jenkin Jones, probably from enfeebled health, did not continue to preach up to the time of his death. The pulpit was supplied by Revs. Isaac Eaton, Isaac Stella, Thomas Davis, B. Griffiths, P. P. Vanhorn, Samuel Stillman, D. D., B. Miller, John Marks, Owen Thomas, Joseph Thomas, Samuel Heaton. There are also records of some bickerings, but, by prudence and counsel, said troubles, were healed. Anxious to obtain a pastor, and there being no one in the country suitable, whom they could secure, March 13, 1760, the church authorized John Griffith, "to write to the Board of Ministers in London, to request that they send us a minister." Another letter also "was sent by the well-wishers" of the church. July 16, 1760, Jenkin Jones died, and his funeral sermon was preached on the 20th by Rev. Isaac Eaton. He was a man who had rendered good service to the cause of Christ, the Baptist denomination and to the church in Philadelphia. He was the means of securing to the Baptists the property on Second Street, when the Episcopalians attempted to get it. He built a parsonage for the church partly at his own expense. He gave a legacy, July 3, 1762, towards purchasing a large silver cup or chalice for the Lord's Table, which cost about £60 Pennsylvania currency. The church on receipt of this legacy, July 3, 1762, "Agreed that M. Edwards and Isaac

Jones, Esq., do buy a two handle silver cup or chalice, for the wine in the Lord's Supper, with the said legacy, and in case the chalice should cost more than £25, that the old silver cup (now belonging to the Meeting) should be sold to help pay for the new chalice. And that the Rev. Jenkin Jones' name be engraved on the front of the new chalice. This is still used by the church at every communion season. On the face of it is the inscription:

>The Legacy of
>The Rev^d
>JENKIN JONES,
>who died, July 16th,
>1760.

In addition to this cup, the church has in use two plates. On the rim of each is the inscription:

>Baptist Church, Philada.
>1753.

On two of the goblets used in the communion service is inscribed:

>The Particular
>Baptist Church
>of
>Philadelphia,
>1794.

Mr. Jones was the moving cause of securing such alterations in the licence laws as to enable dissenting ministers to perform the marriage ceremony. At his death he was buried in the graveyard adjoining the church, where a tomb was erected to his memory. Upon the removal of the dead from that place in 1860, his remains were reinterred in a beautiful spot in Mount Moriah Cemetery.

A letter from London was promptly received in answer to the one sent, recommending Rev. Morgan Edwards, and on September 15th, the church directed a letter to be drawn up inviting "Mr. Edwards to come over, or any other gentleman of like character, to take the ministerial charge of the church." The School at Hopewell was succeeding well and the students were beginning to go abroad to preach. Under date of April 12, 1760, the minutes of the church in Philadelphia state: "The 20th of this month, Mr. Talbot preached with great warmth. He was the first fruit of the Hopewell School." Rev. John Gano was requested to supply the church until the spring, when Mr. Edwards was expected.

In Mr. Gano's autobiography he records the following relative to this request; "During my residence in North Carolina, Mr. Jenkin Jones, pastor of the Baptist Church in Philadelphia, died; and the church being destitute of a pastor, had sent a call to England for one. It was represented that they had been so particular in the requisite qualifications for a minister, that it has given offence to the preachers; so that they were entirely destitute. They made application to me to visit them; and also to Mr. Miller, of Scotch Plains, who had been a successful minister in New York, and had baptized sundry persons there. I visited New York and Philadelphia, alternately. I at length came to the conclusion that I would supply both places, two Sabbaths at each place. The church at Philadelphia invited me to bring my family, and tarry with them, till they received an answer from England. I answered them that I would not come on such terms; but if they would affix a certain time for my stay, I would accept of their invitation. To this proposal they acceded, and I went to Philadelphia. While there, Mrs. Gano had a daughter, born December 23d, 1760, whom we called Peggy. During my stay there, which was through the winter, the church appeared in a flourishing state, and several additions were made to it."

"About the time I left Philadelphia," continues John Gano, "Providence blessed that church, by sending a young and respectable preacher, Samuel Hillman, from South Carolina, among them. He possessed popular talents as a speaker. He continued with them till the arrival of Morgan Edwards, the minister from England. Mr. Stillman went to Boston, where he now continues, pastor of the First Baptist Church in that place. I remained in the city of New York, until the British War."

In connection with the passing events of the denomination, it would be of interest to weave in the various occurrences of importance connected with the mental, and material life of the city. Except where these are so manifestly interwoven with the history of the Baptists, however, the record of them would unnecesarily enlarge the limits of this work.

CHAPTER IX.—1761-1763.

A NEW ERA.—REV. MORGAN EDWARDS ARRIVES.—DR. G. WEED'S SELF-ESTEEM.—EXCOMMUNICATED FOR DRUNKENNESS.—SUPERVISION OF THE MEMBERSHIP.—MORGAN EDWARDS PROMINENT.—ASSOCIATION'S LETTER TO ENGLAND.—NEED OF BOOKS.—FIRST TABLE OF STATISTICS.—BROWN UNIVERSITY PROJECTED.—MORGAN EDWARDS THE PROJECTOR.—EDUCATIONAL GROWTH.—NEW MEETING-HOUSE IN PHILADELPHIA.—ST. MICHAEL'S LUTHERAN CHURCH.—SOUND OF THE ORGAN.—RESIGNATION OF REV. P. P. VANHORN.—THE CITY'S SEAL TO ORDINATION CERTIFICATES.—GEORGE EATON.—SAMUEL JONES BAPTIZED.—LICENSED TO PREACH.—COPY OF THE LICENSE. —ORDAINED.—PLACE OF WORSHIP OCCUPIED.—MR. WHITEFIELD'S CHURCH.—UNIVERSITY OF PENNSYLVANIA.—UNION METHODIST EPISCOPAL CHURCH.—SAMUEL JONES PASTOR AT PENNYPACK.—A PREROGATIVE OF THE MINISTRY.—WEARING A MASTER'S GOWN.— REV. STEPHEN WATTS.—ORDINATION OF DEACONS.

THIS decade ushered in a marked advance in all that pertains to real progress. New men appeared on the stage, and new measures were inaugurated. May 23, 1761, Rev. Morgan Edwards arrived in this city. He was born in Wales, May 9th, 1722, and commenced preaching when sixteen years of age. After completing his labors he served a church in Boston, England, for seven years, then one in Cork, Ireland, for nine years. From Cork, he returned to England, and preached for a year at Rye, in Sussex. During his residence there, Rev. Dr. Gill, of London, received a letter from the church in Philadelphia, requesting him to assist them in obtaining a pastor. He applied to Mr. Edwards as the person most likely to suit and satisfy the people. The application was favorably received and he took passage for America. Upon his arrival he at once entered upon the pastorate of the church, and was received into their fellowship June 1st, by letter from Penyam, in Monmouthshire, South Wales. The church paid the expenses of his voyage and gave to him a very cordial reception. There are men who are very ready to preach simply because of a high estimation of themselves. The First Church had one of these men in its early history. The minutes for September 4th, 1762, state " Dr. G. Weed proposed to preach to us occasionally. The thing was considered and this answer returned, 'The church return our Bro. Weed thanks for his desire to serve the church; but would defer the proposal till they see necessary to invite Mr. Weed thereto.' The Doctor was not pleased, and said it was like a trick which Dr. Faustus played with the devil." This did not quiet him. Having charge of the Hospital, he seemed there to assume ministerial functions, preaching there as a *minister*, without the authority of the church, and inviting persons from without to come and hear him. The church wrote him a kindly but decided letter remonstrating with him, declaring that they "knew Bro. Weed very well, yet are not willing to know Minister Weed." This course displeased the Doctor, and the church, July 1, 1765, was compelled to erase his name from the records for non-attendance on and non-support of the church.

At the church meeting following the above, October 2d, 1762, there was an excommunication, the record of which is not without interest at this date:—

Whereas, John Taylor has now, a third time, contradicted his baptismal vows of repentance and holiness by relapsing to the sin of drunkenness; and has, moreover, absconded from his master, whereby he has defrauded his master out of a year's servitude; we hold ourselves bound to cut him off from the church, erase his name out of the church's book, and deliver him up to Satan for the destruction of the flesh, that the spirit may be saved in the day of the Lord Jesus; and accordingly he is hereby excommunicated. And God have mercy on his soul. Amen.

That a thorough supervision of the members of the church might be maintained, it was agreed, November 6th, 1762, "that Mr. Edwards do give each regular member of this church twelve written tickets every year, and that each communicant put one in the box at every communion, that it may be known who are absent, that an enquiry may be made after them."

Morgan Edwards at once took a prominent position, because of his talents, energy and piety. Accordingly, at the meeting of the Association, succeeding his arrival, he was placed in a position of prominence, trust and work. He was "appointed to take charge of the book of records, and insert therein the minutes," of that body, in connection with Rev. P. P. Vanhorn. This is the work that had been begun by Benjamin Griffiith. He was also appointed one of the librarians of the Association, and of the correspondents with the Baptists in "London and elsewhere."

The letter to England is of value as a historical document, and is as follows:—

The Association of Particular Baptist Churches, annually held at Philadelphia, to the Board of Particular Baptist Ministers in London:

Reverend Brethren, We greet you well; and, as a part of that community, in the British Dominions, (whereof you have in some sort the superintendence,) we offer you our acquaintance, and solicit a share of your public care and friendship. Our numbers in these parts multiply, for when we had the pleasure of writing to you, in 1734, there were but nine churches in our Association, yet now there are twenty-eight, all owning the Confession of Faith put forth in London, in 1689. Some of the churches are now destitute; but we have a prospect of supplies, partly by means of a Baptist academy lately set up. This infant seminary of learning is yet weak, having no more than twenty-four pounds a year towards its support. Should it be in your power to favor this school any way, we presume you will be pleased to know how. A few books proper for such a school, or a small apparatus, or some pieces of apparatus, are more immediately wanted, and not to be had easily in these parts. We have also of late endeavoured to form a library at Philadelphia, for the use of our brethren in the ministry who are not able to purchase books. This design also wants the assistance of our brethren in England. However, our design in writing to you in this public manner is to renew a correspondence which hath been dropped for some years past: and if you think well of it, we shall be glad to hear from you against our next Association, in October. You may direct to our brother, Morgan Edwards, at Philadelphia. We commend you to the grace of God, and desire your prayers for us, and remain your brethren in the faith. Signed, by order of the Association,

         PETER PETERSON VANHORN,
Philadelphia, May 16, 1762. MORGAN EDWARDS.

The effect of the presence of Morgan Edwards is seen in the improved value of the minutes of the Association for that year. For the first time is given, in 1761, a table of statistics of the churches, collected and arranged by him. The Pennypack, Philadelphia and Montgomery churches, all the Baptist churches in the entire country then, reported that year an aggregate membership of 202; total number of baptisms, 30; and entire number of "hearers," 1150.

In "a sketch of the history and the present organization of Brown University, published by the Executive Board," in 1861, is this statement :—

> This Institution, which was founded in 1794, owes its origin to the desire of the Baptists in the American Colonies to secure for members of their denomination a liberal education, without subjection to any sectarian tests. At the suggestion of Rev. Morgan Edwards, the pastor of the First Baptist Church, in Philadelphia, the Philadelphia Baptist Association, in the year 1762, resolved to establish a college in the colony of Rhode Island and Providence plantations. The Rev. James Manning, a graduate of the College of New Jersey, was commissioned by them to travel through the northern colonies, for the purpose of fostering this project.

In 1764, a charter was obtained for the College from the legislature of the colony. Rev. Morgan Edwards was elected a member of its first Board of Fellows, a position which he held until 1789.

With the inauguration of this enterprise, the Philadelphia Association thus earnestly expressed itself in 1764 :—

> Agreed, to inform the churches to which we respectively belong, that, inasmuch as a charter is obtained in Rhode Island government toward erecting a Baptist college, the churches should be liberal in contributing towards carrying the same into execution.

In 1766, this body again

Agreed, to recommend warmly to our churches the interest of the college, for which a subscription is opened all over the continent. This college hath been set on foot upward of a year, and has now in it three promising youths under the tuition of President Manning.

The year in which Brown University was first projected in Philadelphia was signalized by tearing down the Baptist Meeting-house, erected in 1731, in Lagrange Place, and the construction of a more spacious edifice. 61 by 42 feet. Like its predecessor, it was built of brick, and cost £2,200. This rebuilding will, doubtless, account for the fact that the Association, in 1762, "met at the Lutheran church in Fifth street, between Arch and Race streets, where *the sound of the organ* was heard in the Baptist worship." This was St. Michael's Church, at the corner of Fifth and Cherry streets.

February 7th, of this year, Rev. P. P. Vanhorn, after an acceptable pastorate of nearly fifteen years, resigned the care of the Pennypack church, and removed to New Mills, now Pemberton, New Jersey, where, June 23, 1764, he was instrumental in founding the Baptist church. April 2, 1768, he returned to and resided at Pennypack. December 9th, 1769, he was again received into the church and remained a member of it until September 18th, 1770, when he removed to Cape May, New Jersey, and became pastor there. At the Association in 1762, "Certificates of the ordination and good morals of Rev. David Thomas and Rev. David Sutton were drawn up by Rev. Samuel Jones and Isaac Jones, Esq., and the city seal affixed thereto by the Recorder, Benjamin Chew, Esq., for which he took no fee." This seal attached to the aforenamed certificate is a curiosity in this day, when such a custom has fallen into disuse almost entirely. It also contains a high testimony to the Baptist pastor in this city. It is as follows:—

I, Benjamin Chew, Esq., Recorder of the city of Philadelphia, do hereby certify that the Rev. Morgan Edwards, A. M., who hath

NEW MEETING-HOUSE IN PHILADELPHIA.

MEETING-HOUSE OF FIRST BAPTIST CHURCH, LAGRANGE PLACE.

signed the above certificate, is pastor of the Baptist church in this city of Philadelphia, and Moderator of the above Association, and that he s a gentleman of most exemplary morals and piety.

In testimony of which, I have hereunto caused the seal of this said city to be affixed, this 17th day of October, A. D. 1762.

BENJAMIN CHEW, *Recorder*.

After the departure of P. P. Vanhorn to Pemberton, the minutes of the Pennypack church, under date of March 11th, 1762, contain the following :—

Concluded to call Bro. George Eaton to supply us ye remainder of ye time, excepting ye 3rd Sabbath in every month, at which time he is under promise to preach at a place called the Ridge, near Germantown.

The place referred to as "the Ridge," is Roxborough.

Mr. Eaton did not live to labor long after this, as the inscription on the plain, blue marble headstone, which marks his last resting place, in the graveyard at Pennypack, will inform us. It is as follows :—

In memory of
the REV. GEORGE EATON,
who departed this life July
1st, 1764, aged 77 years
11 months.
Who did delight his talents to improve,
And speak ye glorys of Redeeming love.

Mr. Eaton was born in Wales, and was brought to this country in 1686 by his parents when but a litttle babe. He was the brother of Rev. Joseph Eaton, whose son, Isaac, founded the Latin School, at Hopewell, New Jersey.

Samuel Jones, who arrived in this city in 1737, was converted very early in life and became a member of the Tulpehocken Baptist Church in Berks County, Pa., of which his father Rev. Thomas Jones was pastor. Samuel entered upon a course of study in the College of Philadelphia, and December 5, 1760, was received into the Baptist Church of this city by letter from the one at Tulpehocken. He prosecuted his studies until May 18, 1762, when he was graduated and received the degree of Bachelor of Arts. He was shortly thereafter licensed by the church to preach the Gospel. The following is a copy of the license:—

To all whom it may concern. This certifies that Samuel Jones, A. B., has been regularly called to exercise his ministerial gifts by the Baptist Church of Philadelphia, whereof he is a member, and, after trial in private and public, the Church judge he will be useful in the Ministry. Wherefore he is hereby licensed and authorized to preach the Gospel wherever he may have a call so to do among the Baptists, until such time as circumstances will admit of his ordination. Done at a Church Meeting held in the College of Philadelphia July 10, 1762. Signed in behalf of the whole, by us.

MORGAN EDWARDS, *Minister.*
JOSHUA MOOR, GEORGE WESTCOTT, } *Deacons.*
SAMUEL DAVIS, SEPTIMUS LEVERING, }

December 4, 1762, the Church "agreed unanimously that Samuel Jones be ordained on January 2, 1763, and that Messrs. Morgan Edwards, Isaac Eaton and Samuel Stillman be concerned therein, and that messengers be sent to invite the two last to give their attendance. Morgan Edwards to preach the sermon and to conduct the ordination, Isaac Eaton to give the Charge; and all to be concerned in imposition of hands and prayer." The address of the church to these ministering brethren relative to this ordination is of interest:—

To Messrs. Morgan Edwards, Isaac Eaton and Samuel Stillman:—

Rev. Sirs: We, the Baptist Church of Philadelphia, greet you well, and beg leave to recommend to you for ordination cur beloved brother Samuel Jones, A. B., whom we, by our representative, Mr. Wescott, set before you for that purpose. He is a man of sound learning, good morals, and exemplary piety, your compliance with our request will be doing a pleasure to your brethren in the faith and fellowship of the Gospel. Signed by order, and in behalf of the church at our meeting of business in the College of Philadelphia, January 1, 1763.

BARNABY BARNES, *Clerk.*

From the above documents, aside from their interest, we learn that during the rebuilding of the Meeting House on Second Street, the church worshipped in the hall of the

College of Philadelphia. This edifice was on the west side of Fourth Street, below Arch. It was originally erected in 1741, for the Rev. George Whitefield, and was known as Whitefield's Church. In 1749 an Academy and Charitable School was organized in the city, and occupied this building. In 1750 it was opened as a Latin School; in 1755 it was chartered under the title of "The College, Academy, and Charitable School of Philadelphia," and in 1779 was opened as the University of Pennsylvania. The Union Methodist Episcopal Church now occupies the identical spot of Whitefield's Church, or College Hall. Samuel Jones forthwith became pastor of the Pennypack and Southampton Churches, a position he filled until 1770, when he resigned the latter and gave himself exclusively to the pastorship of the former. At the time of his ordination it would seem that the Church in Philadelphia regarded it as the prerogative of the Ministry to determine upon the qualification of a candidate for Baptism. Accordingly the subject was brought up and decided at the Meeting of the Association as follows:—

A question was moved by the church of the Great Valley to this effect: Whether it be the prerogative of a church to receive applications for Baptism, examine the candidates, and to judge of their qualifications for Baptism, or whether these be the distinct and peculiar prerogatives of the Minister, exclusive of the laity?

The occasion of this question was the opinion and practice of the Church of Philadelphia, who by a general vote have allowed the said prerogatives to belong to the Minister, by the tenor of the commission relative to Baptism, and the universal practice of the commissioners; and that there is neither precept nor precedent for the contrary in Scripture. All allowed that this may be, and in some cases must be; but that the other practice was more expedient. However, none pretended to say it was warranted by Scripture. The question was put, —Whether the point was a term of Communion, and whether it should be debated or dropped? None stood up for either. So that it was dropped.

In 1762 the degree of Master of Arts was conferred on Morgan Edwards by the College of Philadelphia, and in

1769 the same honor was bestowed by Brown University. Whether the reception of this degree prompted the action as recorded in the Church Minutes for April 30, 1763, we do not profess to say:—

Mr. Edwards desires to know the sense of the church relative to his wearing a master's gown in the common services of the Church; for as to wearing it abroad and on special occasions, he said, he intended to use his right and own discretion. The Church desired him to use his liberty and that wearing or not wearing it would give no offence to the Church.

June 4, 1763, the church called Stephen Watts, a licentiate and a graduate of the College of Philadelphia, to be an Assistant to Rev. Morgan Edwards in the Ministry. He accepted the call and entered upon the work July 2nd. The ordination of deacons was strictly adhered to by the Churches at this time. An account of such ordination in Philadelphia is given in the Records for December 10, 1763:—

The Church met this day, by way of preparation for celebrating the Lord's Supper on the morrow; and to ordain deacons. The Meeting began with prayer from the desk suitable to both designs of the Meeting. Then was delivered a dissertation on the office of a deacon, his qualifications and duty and the manner of his election and instalment in the office. Then the deacons elect, viz. Joseph Moulder, Joseph Watkins and Samuel Miles were brought to the administrator; who laid his hands on each, and prayed in the following words: In the name of the Lord Jesus, and according to the practice of His Apostles towards persons chosen to the deaconship, I lay hands on you, my brother, whereby you are constituted, or ordained a deacon of this church; installed in the office and appointed and empowered to collect and receive her revenues, and to dispose thereof in providing for and serving the Lord's table; and in providing for the table of the Minister and the poor; and in transacting other temporal affairs of the church, that the Minister may not be deterred from the word and prayer, nor the concerns of the family of faith neglected. In the use of which rite of imposition of hands, I pray that God will confirm in heaven what we do on earth, and receive you into the number of them who minister to him in the civil affairs of His sanctuary. That he will fill you more and more with the Holy Ghost, wisdom and honesty; that, by using the office of a deacon well, you may purchase to yourself a good degree, and great boldness in the faith, even so Lord Jesus. Amen. When each had been ordained, they stood up from kneeling and were addressed by the Minister in the following manner: We give you the right hand of fellowship in token that we acknowledge you for our deacon, and to express our congratulations and good wishes.

CHAPTER X.—1764-1770.

THE SISTERS ALLOWED TO VOTE.—RULING ELDERS.—FRATERNAL ASSOCIATIONAL CORRESPONDENCE.—WARREN ASSOCIATION ORGANIZED.—LETTER FROM PHILADELPHIA.—RHODE ISLAND COLLEGE AND MORGAN EDWARDS.—DEATH OF REV. BENJAMIN GRIFFITH.—FIRST COMMENCEMENT OF BROWN UNIVERSITY.—MINUTES FIRST PRINTED.—NORTHERN LIBERTIES CHURCH.—PERSECUTIONS.—PHILADELPHIA ASSOCIATION TO THE RESCUE.—SUFFERINGS AT ASHFIELD.—NEW MEETING-HOUSE AT PENNYPACK.

UNDER date of March 13, 1764, a new phase of church polity was introduced. For some years the sisters had not taken part in the business of the church. While the names of the brethren are given who were present at each business meeting, no ladies are mentioned as attending. On the above date, the following question was, "on behalf of some of the sisters" propounded: "Whether women have a right to vote in church affairs?" On March 31st, an answer was returned, " with due honor to the sisters," as follows:—

That the rights of Christians are not subject to our determinations, nor to the determinations of any church or state upon earth. We could easily answer that, in civil affairs, they have no such right; but whether they have or have not in the church, can only be determined by the Gospel, to which we refer them. But, if, upon inquiry, no such grant of right can be found in the Gospel, and if voting shall appear to be a mere custom, we see no necessity for breaking it except the custom should, at any time, be stretched to subvert the subordination which the Gospel hath established in all the churches of the saints, "I suffer not a woman to usurp authority, but command that she be in subjection, as also saith the law." 1 Tim. 2. 1., 1 Cor. 14. Nor do we know that this church, or any of us, have done anything to deprive the sisters of such a practice, be it a right, or be it a custom only, except a neglect on a late occasion be deemed such, which we justify not. On the contrary, if the sisters do attend our meetings of business, we propose that their suffrage or disapprobation shall have their proper influence; and, in case they do not attend statedly, we purpose to invite them when anything is to be transacted which touches the interest of their souls.

May 5th, a communication was received from the women in reply, and it was decided that the sisters should have the right of suffrage as in former years.

Like the church at Pennypack, the one in Philadelphia had Ruling Elders. Three were elected for the first time May 10th, 1866. Their names were Isaac Jones, George Westcott and Samuel Davis. June 14th, "they were ordained by laying on of hands and prayer."

In 1766, was commenced that fraternal correspondence on the part of the Philadelphia Association which, for so many years, was carried on, and from which in the early days so much of pleasure and encouragement resulted. It was then

> Moved and agreed to: That a yearly intercourse between the Associations to the east and west of us be, by letters and messengers, now begun, and hereafter maintained. Accordingly, Rev. Samuel Jones was ordered to write to the Association to be held at Warren, the Tuesday before the second Sunday in September, and Revs. John Gano, Samuel Jones and Morgan Edwards appointed to meet them as delegates from us.

This was the first meeting of the Warren Association, at the organization of which the number of Baptist Associations in the country had increased to seven, viz: the Philadelphia, organized in 1707; the Charleston, in South Carolina, 1751; the Sandy Creek, in North Carolina, 1758; the Leyden, in Massachusetts, 1763; the Kuhukee, in North Carolina, 1765; the Ketockton, in Virginia, 1766; and the Warren, in Rhode Island, 1767.

Up to 1766 the Baptist Churches of New England had not been gathered into an Association. Rev. James Maning was exceedingly anxious that this should be done. A meeting for this purpose was held at Warren, Rhode Island, September 8, 1767. From the Philadelphia Association were Rev. John Gano (who preached the introductory sermon from Acts xv: 9, and was chosen Moderator of the new body), Rev. Abel Griffith, and Noah Hammond. The following letter was sent by them :—

The Elders and Messengers of the several Baptist Churches met in Association at Philadelphia, the 14th, 15th, and 16th day of October, 1766. To the Elders and Messengers of the several Baptist Churches of the same faith and order, to meet in Association at Warren, in the Colony of Rhode Island, the 8th day of September, 1767, send greeting. Dearly Beloved Brethren:—When we understood that you concluded to meet at the time and place above mentioned, with a view to lay the foundation stone of an associational building, it gave us peculiar joy, in that it opened to our view a prospect of much good being done. You will perhaps judge this our address to you premature, because as yet you have only an *ideal* being, as a body by appointment. But if you should call this our forwardness blind zeal, we are still in hopes you will not forget that our embracing the first opportunity of commencing Christian fellowship and acquaintance with you affords the strongest evidence of our approbation of your present meeting, and how fond we should be of mutual correspondence between us in this way.

A long course of experience and observation has taught us to have the highest sense of the advantages which accrue from associations ; nor indeed does the nature or thing speak any other language. For, as particular members are collected together and united in one body, which we call a particular church, to answer those ends and purposes which could not be accomplished by any single member, so a collection and union of churches into one associational body may easily be conceived capable of answering those still greater purposes which any particular church could not be equal to. And by the same reason, a union of associations will still increase the body in weight and strength, and make it good that a three-fold cord is not easily broken.

Great, dear brethren, is the design of your meeting, great is the work which lies before you. You will need the guidance and influence of the Divine Spirit, as well as the exertion of all prudence and wisdom. It is therefore our most ardent prayer that you may meet in love, that peace and unanimity may subsist among you during your consultations, that you may be animated with zeal for the glory of God, and directed to advise and determine what may most conduce to promote the Redeemer's Kingdom.

From considering the divided state of our Baptist Churches in your quarters, we foresee that difficulties may arise, such as may call for the exercise of the greatest tenderness and moderation, that if happy, through the blessing of God on your endeavors, those lesser differences may subside, and a more general union commence.

As touching our consultations at this, our meeting, the minutes of our proceedings (a printed copy whereof we shall herewith enclose) will inform you, and if in anything further you should be desirous of information with regard to us, we refer you to our reverend and beloved brethren Morgan Edwards, John Gano and Samuel Jones, who as our representative delegates, will present you with this our letter, and whom we recommend to Christian fellowship with you. And now dear brethren, farewell. May the Lord bless and direct you in all things, and grant that we may all hereafter form one general assembly at his right hand, through infinite riches of free grace in Christ Jesus our Lord. Signed by order and in behalf of the Association, by

BENJAMIN MILLER, *Moderator.*
SAMUEL JONES, *Clerk.*

Realizing the importance of and the necessity for the Rhode Island College, and as funds were needed, both for the support of the institution and for the ultimate erection of a suitable College building, Morgan Edwards, who had this subject right on his heart, was released by his people from the care of his church for a time, his pulpit being supplied by the different ministers of the Association, in order that he might collect the needed aid for the College. These ministers were compensated out of the salary of Mr. Edwards. This act was generous on the part of his church, the ministering brethren, and Mr. Edwards, and exhibited the warm place that education held in their hearts. In 1767, he visited England and Ireland, for the purpose of soliciting funds. His subscription paper bearing the honored names of Benjamin Franklin and Benjamin West, may still be seen in the college archives. On his relation to this Institution Dr. William Rogers, in his sermon commemorative of Morgan Edwards, well said:—

The College of Rhode Island is greatly beholden to him for his vigorous exertions, at home and abroad, in raising money for that Institution, and for his particular activity in procuring its charter. This he deemed the greatest service he ever did for the honor of the Baptist name. As one of its first sons, I cheerfully make this public testimony of his laudable and well-timed zeal.

One week before the meeting of the Association, in 1768, the venerable and faithful Benjamin Griffith, of Montgomery, fell asleep in Jesus. This was on October 5th, in the eighty-first year of his age. In his day he was one of the prominent men of the denomination. Morgan Edwards says, "Mr. Griffith was a man of parts, though not eloquent, and had by industry acquired tolerable acquaintance with languages and books." He states also that he was once offered a commission of Justice of the Peace, which, however, he declined; and on being asked the reason why he refused such an honor, he replied, "men are not to receive from offices, but offices from men—as much as men receive the others lose, till at last offices come to have no honor at all."

The Philadelphia Association usually met in this city, though in its earlier years it may have met occasionally at Pennypack, Piscataway, Cohansey, Middleton, and Welsh Tract. The first record of its meeting out of this city is in 1769, when its sessions were held in New York, with the church constituted there June 19, 1762. At this meeting held in October, pleasing accounts from Rhode Island College were conveyed to the Association. Its first Commencement had been held the previous month, when seven young men had been graduated, among whom was William Rogers, hereafter to be mentioned. The College was very profuse in its honors that year, twenty-two Ministers or laymen receiving honorary degrees, among those who were the recipients of the Master's degree were Rev. Morgan Edwards, Samuel Jones, John Davis and Abel Morgan of the Philadelphia Association. Whether these honors had the effect to lead the Association to appreciate the importance of having their Minutes printed we are not informed; at any rate, that year, for the first time, the Minutes were printed for distribution among the churches. "Morgan Edwards," says Dr. Rogers, "was the moving cause of having the Minutes of the Philadelphia Association printed,

G

which he could not bring to bear for some years, and therefore at his own expense he printed tables, exhibiting the original and annual state of the Associating Churches." In the Minutes for that year is the following record:—

> It was shown by some from Philadelphia, that they had obtained leave from the church they belonged to, (on Second Street) to form themselves into a distinct society in the Northern Liberties of that city, and they were desirous to know the sense of the Association touching their design; voted, That if any of our Ministers were free to constitute them into a church, in said Liberties, they might do it without offending the Association.

This answer would imply that there was some doubt as to the propriety of this movement, yet the church was organized, as in the Minutes of the next year is the following:—

> The church in the Northern Liberties, of Philadelphia, proposed to join the Association; but, objections being made, the matter was referred to the Committee, who brought in their report, and the junction was deferred.

By this time the churches and members of our denomination, who had already endured such bitter persecutions in New England, Virginia and other places, were growing restless under the fierce hostilities for non-conformity to the religious establishments. They came with a statement of their wrongs to the Philadelphia Association, and that body, loyal to the great Baptist principle of liberty of conscience, then, as ever afterward, manifested practical sympathy, and inaugurated those active measures which contributed their influence in securing to this country, ultimately, that religious liberty now enjoyed. The minutes for 1769 state:—

> By letter and messengers from Warren, we were informed that they had petitioned the Legislatures of Boston and Connecticut in favor of their brethren who suffer for non-conformity to the religious establishments of those colonies; and in case their petitions produced not a speedy or effectual redress of their grievances, requested that we would join with them in a petition to our gracious sovereign.

Voted, that this Association will not only join that of Warren in seeking relief for our oppressed brethren, but will also solicit the concurrence of the Associations of Virginia and Carolina in the design, if need be.

Voted also, That letters and messengers be sent to signify this, our resolution. The letter to the Warren Association was drawn up by the Rev. Samuel Jones; the messengers, Rev. Samuel Waldo and Rev. Benjamin Coles. That to the Virginia Association by Rev. Hezekiah Smith; the messenger, Rev. John Gano.

These efforts were unavailing, however, as we learn from the Association minutes of 1770 :—

By the letter from the Warren Association, it appears that our brethren in New England are sorely oppressed this year again, and no redress obtained, though diligently sought for; their case is to go home soon, to be laid at the feet of our gracious sovereign. Rev. Hezekiah Smith is appointed agent, who proposes to sail about the beginning of November. They requested their brethren belonging to this Association to help them to defray the expenses of the agent. The request was attended to with much sympathy. Collections to be made in all our churches immediately and to be sent either to Mr. George Wescott, of Philadelphia, or Mr. Williams, of New York, to be by them forwarded to London. Also, a committee was appointed to draw a memorial, addressed to Rev. Dr. Stennett and others, in favor of our New England brethren's design.

We cannot here refrain from giving the contents of the letters received from New England concerning the sufferings of our brethren at Ashfield, near Boston :—

The laws of this province were never intended to exempt the Baptists from paying towards building and repairing Presbyterian meeting-houses, and making up Presbyterian ministers' salaries; for, besides other insufficiencies, they are all limited as to extent and duration. The first law extended only five miles around each Baptist meeting-house; those without this circle had no relief, neither had they within, for, though it exempted their polls, it left their estate to the mercy of harpies, and their estates went to wreck. The Baptists sought a better law, and with great difficulty, and waste of time and money, obtained it. But this was not universal; it extended not to any parish until a Presbyterian meeting-house should be built and a Presbyterian minister settled there; in consequence of which, the Baptists have never been freed from the first and great expenses of their parishes—expenses equal to the current expenses of ten or twelve years. This is the present case of the people of Ashfield, which is a Baptist settlement. There were but five families of other denominations in the place when the Baptist church was constituted; but those five and a few more have lately built a Presbyterian meeting-house and settled an orthodox minister, as they call him; which last cost £200. To pay for both, they laid a tax on the land, and, as the Baptists are the most numerous, the greatest part fell to their share. The Presbyterians, in April last demanded the money. The Baptists pleaded poverty, alleging that they had been twice driven from their plantations by the Indians' last war; that they were but new settlers, and had cleared but a few spots of land, and had not been able to build commodious dwelling houses. The tyrants would not hear. Then the Baptists pleaded the ingratitude of such conduct, for they had built a fort there at their own expense, and had maintained it for two years, and so had protected the interior Presbyterians, as well as their neighbors, who now rose up against them; that the Baptists to the westward had raised money to relieve Presbyterians who had, like them, suffered from the Indians; and that it was cruel to take from them what the Indians had left. But nothing touched the hearts of these cruel people. Then the Baptists urged the law of the province; but were soon told that that law extended to no new parish till the meeting-house and minister were paid for. Then the Baptists petitioned the general court; proceedings were stopped till further orders, and the poor people went home rejoicing, thinking their property safe, but had not all got home before said order came, and it was an order for the Presbyterians to proceed. Accordingly, in the month of April they fell foul on their plantations, and not on skirts and corners, but on the cleared and improved spots, and so have mangled their estates, and left them hardly any but a wilderness; they sold the house and garden of one man, and the young orchards, meadows and corn-fields of others; nay, they sold their dead, for they sold their grave-yard. The orthodox minister was one of the purchasers. These spots amounted to three hundred and ninety-five acres, and have since been valued at £363 8s., but were sold for £35 10s. This was the first payment; two more are coming, which will not leave them an inch of land at this rate. The Baptists waited on the Assembly five times this year for relief, but were not heard, under pretence they did no business; but their enemies were heard, and had their business done. At last the Baptists got together about a score of the members at Cambridge, and made their complaint known; but in general they were treated very superciliously. One of them spoke to this effect: "*The general assembly have a right to do what they did, and if you don't like it you may quit the place.*" But, alas, they must leave their all behind! These Presbyterians are not only supercilious in power, but mean and cruel in mastery. When they came together to mangle the estates of the Baptists, they diverted themselves with the tears and lamentations of the oppressed. One of them, whose name is Wells, stood up to preach a mock sermon on the occasion; and, among other things, used words to this effect: "*The Baptists, for refusing to pay an orthodox minister, shall be cut in pound pieces and boiled for their fat to grease the devil's carriage,*" etc.

The meeting-house at Pennypack, erected in 1707, was torn down in 1770, and a neat stone building was erected, 30 by 33 feet, "with pews, galleries, and a stove, which latter accommodation was not to be found in all the meeting-houses." The present edifice at Lower Dublin was erected in 1805, when Dr. Samuel Jones was pastor.

CHAPTER XI.—1771-1775.

A DECADE OF TRIAL.—REV. MORGAN EDWARDS RESIGNS.—REV. SAMUEL STILLMAN CHOSEN PASTOR.—DID NOT ACCEPT.—NORTHERN LIBERTY CHURCH IN THE ASSOCIATION.—THE MISSIONARY SPIRIT.—MORGAN EDWARDS AN EVANGELIST.—REV. WILLIAM ROGERS ORDAINED.—LAST SERMON OF REV. ISAAC EATON.—DIVINE BLESSING.—JOHN LEVERING.—LAYING ON OF HANDS.—REV. EBENEZER KINNERSLEY RESIGNS HIS PROFESSORSHIP.—DEATH AND BURIAL OF MR. KINNERSLEY.—MEMORIAL WINDOW.—PERSECUTIONS OF BAPTISTS.—ASSOCIATION MEETING TWICE A YEAR.—ACADEMY AT PENNYPACK.—BURGISS ALLISON.—CARPENTER'S HALL.—CONTINENTAL CONGRESS.—REV. ISAAC BACKUS —DIARY OF BACKUS IN PHILADELPHIA.—COMMITTEE OF GRIEVANCES IN THE ASSOCIATION.—MEETING AT CARPENTER'S HALL.—ADDRESS BY REV. JAMES MANNING.—MASSACHUSETTS DELEGATES UNFRIENDLY.—BAPTISTS AND SOUL LIBERTY.—PREJUDICED OPINION OF JOHN ADAMS.—COMMITTEE DETERMINED.—PRINTED DOCUMENTS.—FASTING AND PRAYER.—REV. WILLIAM ROGERS RESIGNED.

WE come now to the decade in American History which tried men's souls, and in which our own city acted no unimportant part. The record of our denomination in these parts then was true and our Ministry almost to a man were loyal to those principles for which, through all the ages of Christianity, Baptists have so earnestly contended. Up to April 6, 1771, Rev. Samuel Jones remained connected with the First Baptist Church; on that date he united with Pennypack. At the church meeting in Philadelphia, held July 8th, 1771, Rev. Morgan Edwards made the following proposal:—

> My Brethren:—I have observed, for some time, that the interest does not thrive under my ministration as it was wont to do in years past, but is rather declining. This has given me trouble, and trouble that I am less able to bear of any other trouble whatsoever. Accordingly, I have the last year made this proposal to some of the Brethren, viz.: that they should look out for a popular Preacher, and that I would resign half my salary in order to enable the church to pay him. Things are still in the same situation, and my declining age and the

present posture of affairs forbid me to hope for better times. I therefore now repeat to the church what I before mentioned to individuals, viz.: that you will seek for a Minister suitable to the place; and a man of such talents as promise the revival of the interest. On this I am much in earnest, and, because in earnest, I do offer you my help to find such a man, either in America or Europe, and to bring him hither. I also propose to insist on no terms for myself which will hinder such an event from coming to pass, and in the meantime intend not to leave you destitute, because I seek your good, as a Church, and the good of the interest in general more than my own private advantage, for the credibility of this I appeal to my whole conduct since I have been here and to my former and present proposal.

This resignation was accepted unconditionally. At the church meeting in August, Rev. Samuel Stillman, and John Davis of Boston, Hezekiah Smith of Haverhill, John Gano of New York, Samuel Jones of Pennypack, and Oliver Hart of Charleston, were placed in nomination for the pastorate. The first one was chosen, and a very urgent and cordial letter was sent to him, to which, while on a visit to this city, he replied as follows:—

To the Baptist Church and Congregation in Philadelphia. Dear Brethren:—Your call I have received and deliberately considered. The application to me, on this occasion, I view as an expression of your affection for and confidence in me, for which I am much obliged to you. Permit me to assure you that I am sensibly touched with your circumstances, and may God send you a pastor after his own heart. The arguments with which you urge your invitation to me are weighty, and would be sufficient to incline me to accept it and settle among you, were I not so closely connected in Boston. A few hints out of many that might be given cannot fail of convincing you that it is impracticable for me to leave a people with whom I am so intimately and agreeably connected. It may suffice to say that the Lord hath been pleased to succeed my imperfect services among the people, insomuch that the church has greatly increased and is now increasing. I left a considerable number under solemn concern of mind. They are also at peace among themselves, and have, for several years, discovered a warm affection for me. The congregation has become so numerous that they have been obliged to pull down the old meeting house and to build one much larger. This house they are now building for me at a great expense, which they cheerfully endure, confiding in me that I will continue among them. Under these circumstances I cannot think it my duty, brethren, to leave them, although it would afford me great pleasure to reside in this my native city, among my relations and friends, and to serve you in the Gospel. Wishing you grace, mercy and peace from Christ Jesus, I subscribe yours in the Faith and Fellowship of the Gospel.

Philadelphia, November 5, 1771.   SAMUEL STILLMAN.

The same year, October 16th, the Northern Liberty Church, referred to in the previous chapter, was received into the Association with sixteen members. Its numbers never increased, and it was supplied with preaching by the ministers of the Association. Its name appears on the Minutes until 1776, but not thereafter. At this session of the Association, the missionary spirit, which, from the very first of its history, had been so manifest in the readiness to visit destitute churches and settlements culminated in the appointment of Rev. Morgan Edwards as an Evangelist. He was "sent into remote regions, especially South, to preach the Gospel, counsel the feeble churches, and instruct the scattered disciples of Christ." This took him from the pastorate which for ten years he had ably filled, and during which time he had baptized into the fellowship of the church one hundred and seventeen persons. The Association Minutes for 1774 state: "The ministers expressed a readiness to supply Philadelphia in case Mr. Edwards should proceed in the execution of his public office." That his work was successful and appreciated is evident, because in 1772, "the thanks of the Association were returned to brother Morgan Edwards for his services in travelling and visiting the churches to the southward; and the interest of the Association fund, for the last year, voted him, together with £6 more, made up by the brethren present, and sent him by Mr. Samuel Jones." January 1, 1770, Rev. Morgan Edwards preached a New Year's sermon from the text, "This year thou shalt die." He became possessed of the idea that on a certain day of that year he would die, which, together with some other irregularities, had an injurious effect, and discouraged him in his pastorate, but he continued preaching for the Church, until the settlement of his successor, an event which in part he was the means of bringing about, in connection with Dr. Stillman. In 1772, he removed with his family to Newark, Delaware, but still retained his connection with the church he had recently served.

In December, 1771, William Rogers, Principal of an Academy at Newport, Rhode Island, was induced to visit Philadelphia, and continued preaching for the church until March 4th, 1772, when he was unanimously called to the pastorate. This he accepted, and was ordained on Sunday, the 31st of May, following. Mr. Rogers was born in Newport, R. I. July 22, 1751. His parents were members of the Baptist Church in that town. Having gone through a preparatory course in Grafton, Mass., he entered the Freshman Class of Brown University, in September, 1765, and graduated with the first class from that institution in 1769. The following year he was converted to God, was baptized by Rev. Gardiner Thurston, and was received as a member of the Second Baptist Church of Newport, *by prayer and the imposition of hands.* In August, 1771, this Church licensed him to preach the Gospel, and dismissed him by letter to Philadelphia, April 14, 1772. The sermon on the occasion of his ordination was preached by Rev. Isaac Eaton, from the words, "Who is sufficient for these things?" This was the last sermon he ever preached, for he died July 4th, 1772, and this text was the first one that Mr. Rogers ever preached from. When we remember that Isaac Eaton was the first Baptist to found an Academy in America, from which really sprang Brown University, also that William Rogers was a member of the first graduating class of that University, it was eminently appropriate that the above sermon should be preached by Mr. Eaton in the very church edifice where Brown University was practically projected. It was singular that the last sermon of this good and useful educator among the Baptists of this country should have been delivered amidst circumstances of such peculiar interest.

God's blessing attended the settlement of Mr. Rogers, from the very first, for, on the 8th of June following his ordination, five persons narrated their experience for baptism, one of these, John Levering, was the first person baptized by Mr. Rogers. He became a constituent member and for forty years an honored deacon of the Roxborough Baptist Church, of this city. By the following October twenty-three persons had been received into the First Church by baptism, and the membership increased to one hundred and sixty-four. It was the custom of the church then, as previously, to admit all members after baptism "by prayer and laying on of hands."

October 17, 1772, Rev. Ebenezer Kinnersley, on account of failing health, tendered his resignation as Professor of Rhetoric in the University of Pennsylvania. His resignation was accepted, and on the minutes of the Board of Trustees of the University, under date of February 23, 1773, is the following record:—

> The College suffers greatly since Mr. Kinnersley left it, for want of a person to teach public speaking, so that the present class have not those opportunities to declaim and speak which have been of so much use to their predecessors, and have contributed greatly to aid the credit of the Institution.

He died July, 1778, and was buried in the grave-yard at Pennypack. His tombstone bears the following simple inscription:—

In memory of the
Rev. Ebenezer Kinnersley,
who died July 4, 1778,
aged 67 years.

A memorial window to his memory has been placed in one of the buildings of the University.

The persecutions of the Baptists in Massachusetts still continued. The letter from the Warren to the Philadelphia Association, in 1773, stated, " Our sufferings in Boston government on religious accounts still continue in several places; a particular narrative of which is to be printed, with a fair representation of the treatment which the Baptists have met with in said government in time past." For these persecuted Baptists of New England, their brethren in Philadelphia ever felt the deepest interest, and manifested the most profound sympathy.

That year, in order that the scattered churches of the Association might more easily reach the sessions, it was resolved, thereafter, that said body should hold two meetings a year, one in May, in New York, and the other in October, in Philadelphia. This plan was carried into effect in 1774, but it was not found practical, so, at the meeting in October, the project was annulled.

Rev. Samuel Jones, of Pennypack, in connection with his ministerial work, commenced an academy in his own residence, for the instruction of young men in theology. Several of our early ministers received their first instruction in divinity there. Among these were Burgis Allison, who was born in Bordentown, N. J., August 17th, 1753, and baptized at Upper Freehold, in the same state, in October, 1769. In 1774 he repaired to the school of Mr. Jones' where he received a classical, and, to some extent, a theological education. June 1st, 1776, he was received by letter into the Pennypack church, by which he was licensed to preach April 27th, 1777. He was ordained there June 10th, 1781, and became pastor of the newly organized church in his native town.

September 5th, 1774, the first Continental Congress met in Philadelphia, at Carpenter's Hall. The grievances of the brethren in New England had become so severe that it was concluded to lay the matter before that body. At a meeting of representatives of twenty Baptist churches, held at Medfield, near Boston, September 14th, Rev. Isaac Backus was selected to proceed to Philadelphia, for this object.

CARPENTER'S HALL.

"Mr. Backus," says Hovey, in his "Life and Times" of this indefatigable laborer for soul liberty, "began his journey on the 26th of September; it occupied nearly a fortnight. At Providence he met with Elders Gano and Van Horne, who went on with him by land. Old Mr. Chileab Smith joined them at Norwich, prepared to testify of the oppressions at Ashfield. On the 8th of October they arrived in Philadelphia, and Mr. Backus was kindly entertained at the house of Mr. Samuel Davis. On the morrow, it being the Lord's day, he preached three times in the pulpit of Rev. William Rogers. His diary indicates sufficiently the course of events during the next few days ":---

"Monday, October 10th, visited Robert Strettle Jones, Esq., in the forenoon, and Mr. Joseph Moulder in the afternoon—gentlemen who were desirous of knowing how our affairs were in New England, and who seem willing to exert themselves in our favor.

"Oct. 11th, our Elders Manning and Jones arrived with others, and we held a meeting at Esquire Jones' in the evening, where were Israel and James Pemberton and Joseph Fox, principal men among the Quakers, with other gentlemen. I then laid open our condition in New England, and asked their advice, whether to lay the case before Congress or not. They advised us not to address Congress as a body, at present, but to seek for a conference with the Massachusetts delegates, together with some other members who were known to be friendly to religious liberty. They also manifested a willingness to be helpful in our case."

"Oct. 12th, spent the forenoon with Esquire Jones in drawing up a memorial of our case to lay before the conference. In the afternoon the Philadelphia Association met in that city, continuing in session three days. Before closing it, made choice of a committee of grievances to correspond with ours in New England, and to prosecute such measures for our relief as they should judge best."

The proceedings of the Association on this matter are thus given in the minutes :—

The case of our brethren suffering under ecclesiastical oppression in New England being taken into consideration, it was agreed to recommend our churches to contribute to their necessities, agreeable to the pattern of the primitive churches, who contributed to the relief of the distressed brethren in Judea. And that the money raised for them be remitted to Mr. Backus, to be by him, in conjunction with the committee of advice in said colony, distributed to the brethren.

The case of our brethren above considered, induced us to appoint a committee of grievances, who may, from time to time, receive accounts of the sufferings and difficulties of our friends and brethren in the neighboring colonies; and meet as often as shall appear needful in the city of Philadelphia, to consult upon and prosecute such measures for their relief as they shall judge most expedient; and may correspond with the Baptist committee in the Massachusetts Bay, or elsewhere. Accordingly, the following gentlemen were appointed, viz.: Robert Strettle Jones, Esq., Mr. Samuel Davis, Mr. Stephen Shewel, Mr. Thomas Shields, Mr. George Wescott, Alexander Edwards, Esq., Benjamin Bartholomew, Esq., John Evans, Esq., John Mayhew, Esq., Edward Keasley, Esq., Rev. Samuel Jones, A.M., Rev. Morgan Edwards, A. M., Rev. William Vanhorn, A. M., Mr. Abraham Beakley, Abel Evans, Esq., Samuel Miles, Esq., Mr. James Morgan and Mr. John Jarman. Any five of them to be a quorum.

"October 14th," says Backus, in his diary, "in the evening, there met at Carpenter's Hall Thomas Cushing, Samuel Adams and Robert Treat Paine, Esqs., delegates from Massachusetts; and there were also present James Kinzie, of New Jersey; Stephen Hopkins and Samuel Ward, of Rhode Island; Joseph Galloway and Thomas Mifflin, Esq., of Pennsylvania; and other members of Congress. Mr. Rhodes, Mayor of the city of Philadelphia, Israel and James Pemberton, and Joseph Fox, Esqrs., of the Quakers, and other gentlemen, also Elders Manning, Gano, Jones, Rogers, Edwards, etc., were present. The conference was opened by Mr. Manning, who made a short speech, and then read the memorial which was drawn up."

This very important historical document, drawn up in Philadelphia, is as follows:—

It has been said by a celebrated writer in politics, that but two things were worth contending for,—Religion and Liberty. For the latter we are at present nobly exerting ourselves through all this extensive continent, and surely no one whose bosom feels the patriot glow in behalf of civil liberty, can remain torpid to the more ennobling flame of RELIGIOUS FREEDOM. The free exercise of private judgment and the unalienable rights of conscience, are of too high a rank and dignity to be subjected to the decrees of councils, or the imperfect laws of fallible legislators. The merciful Father of mankind is the alone Lord of conscience. Establishments may be able to confer worldly distinctions, but cannot create Christians. They have been reared by craft or power, but liberty never flourished perfectly under their control. That liberty, virtue and public happiness can be supported without them, this flourishing province [Pennsylvania] is a glorious testimony, and a view of it would be sufficient to invalidate all the most elaborate arguments ever adduced in support of them. Happy in the enjoyment of these undoubted rights, and conscious of their high import, every lover of mankind must be desirous, as far as opportunity offers, of extending and securing the enjoyment of these inestimable blessings.

These reflections have arisen from considering the unhappy situation of our brethren, the Baptists, in the province of Massachusetts Bay, for whom we now appear as advocates, and from the important light in which liberty in general is now beheld, we trust our representation will be effectual. The province of Massachusetts Bay, being settled by persons who fled from civil and religious oppression, it would be natural to imagine them deeply impressed with the value of liberty, and nobly scorning a domination of conscience. But such was the complexion of the times, they fell from the unhappy state of being oppressed, to the more deplorable and ignoble one of becoming oppressors. But these things being passed over, we intend to begin with the charter obtained at the happy restoration. This charter grants that there shall be liberty of conscience allowed in the worship of God, to all Christians except Papists, inhabiting or which shall inhabit or be resident within this province or territory, or in the words of the late Governor Hutchinson, "We find nothing in the new charter of an ecclesiastical constitution. Liberty of conscience is granted to all except ' Papists.' " The first General Court that met under this charter returned their thanks for the following sentiment delivered before them:—That the magistrate is most properly the officer of human society, that a Christian by nonconformity to this or that imposed way of worship, does not break the terms upon which he is to enjoy the benefits of human society, and that a man has a right to his estate, his liberty, and his family, notwithstanding his nonconformity. And on this declaration the historian who mentions it, plumes himself as if the whole future system of an impartial administration was to begin. By laws made during the first charter, such persons only were entitled to vote for civil rulers as were church members. This might be thought by some to give a shadow of ecclesiastical power; but by the present [charter] "every freeholder of thirty pounds sterling per annum, and every other inhabitant who has forty pounds personal estate, are voters for representatives." So there seems an evident foundation to presume they are only elected for the preservation of civil rights, and the management of temporal concernments. Nevertheless they soon began to assume the power of establishing Congregational worship, and taxed all the inhabitants towards its support, and no act was passed to exempt other denominations from the year 1692 to 1727, when the Episcopalians were permitted to enjoy their rights.

The first act for the relief of the Baptists was in 1728, when their polls only were exempted from taxation, and not their estates, and then only of such as lived within five miles of a Baptist Meeting House. The next year, 1729, thirty persons were apprehended and confined in Bristol Jail, some Churchmen, some Friends, but most of the Baptist denomination. Roused by these oppressions, the Baptists and Quakers petitioned the General Court; being determined, if they could not obtain redress, to apply to his Majesty in council. Wherefore the same year, a law was passed exempting their estates and polls; but clogged however with a limitation, for less than five years. At the expiration of this act, in 1733, our brethren were obliged again to apply to the General Assembly, upon which a third act was passed, 1734, exempting Baptists from paying ministerial taxes. This third act was more clear, accurate and better drawn than any of the former, but for want of a penalty on the returning officer, badly executed, subjecting our brethren to many hardships and oppressions. This act expired in 1740, and another was made for seven years, but still liable to the same defects. In 1747 the Baptists and Friends, wearied with fruitless applications to the assemblies, once more proposed applying at home for relief, when the laws exempting them were reënacted for ten years, the longest space ever granted. To show what the liberty was that these unhappy people enjoyed, it will be necessary, though we aim as much as possible at brevity, just to mention that if at any time a Baptist sued a collector for the breach of these laws, any damages he recovered were laid on the town and the Baptists residing therein were thereby obliged to pay their proportionate part towards his indemnification. At this time such an instance occurred in the case of Sturbridge, when Jonathan Perry sued the collector, Jonathan Mason, and the damages were sustained by the town, though the Baptists in town meeting dissented. And here it may not be improper to observe, that the judges and jury are under the strangest bias to determine for the defendants. In the beginning of the year 1759, an act was passed, breaking in upon the time limited, enacting that "no minister or member of an Anabaptist Church shall be esteemed qualified to give certificates, other than such as shall have obtained, from three other churches commonly called Anabaptist, in this or the neighboring Provinces, a certificate from each respectively, that they esteem such church of their denomination, and that they conscientiously believe them to be Anabaptist.

But not to take too much of your time, we would here just observe that all the laws have been made temporary, and without any penalty on the collector or assessors for the breach of the law passed at the last June session, as it has been generally understood to be so formed as to take away complaint and establish a general liberty of conscience, this act is like all others, temporary, and indeed limited to a shorter duration than most of them, being only for three years. It is without any penalty on the breach of it, and an additional trouble and expense is enjoined by recording the certificates every year, (though in some others obtaining one certificate during the existence of the law was sufficient) and concludes thus: 'that nothing in this act shall be construed to exempt any proprietor of any new township from paying his part and portion with the major part of the other proprietors of such new townships, in settling a minister and building a meeting-house, which hath been or shall be required as a condition of their grant.

And here we would just add a few words relative to the affairs at Ashfield. On the 26th day of December next, three lots of land belonging to people of our denomination, will be exposed for sale; one of them for the payment of so small a sum as ten shillings eleven pence. Although we have given but two instances of oppression under the above laws, yet a great number can be produced, well attested when called for.

Upon this short statement of facts we would observe, that the charter must be looked upon by every impartial eye to be infringed, so soon as any law was passed for the establishment of any particular mode of worship. All Protestants are planted upon the same footing, and no law whatever could disannul so essential a part of a charter intended to communicate the blessings of a free goverment to his Majesty's subjects. Under the first charter, as was hinted, church-membership conferred the rights of a freeman; but by the second, the possession of property was the foundation. Therefore, how could it be supposed that the collective body of the people intended to confer any other power upon their representatives than that of making laws relative to property and the concerns of this life.

"Men unite in society," according to the great Mr. Locke, "with an intention in every one the better to preserve himself, his liberty and property. The power of the society, or Legislature constituted by them, can never be supposed to extend any further than the common good, but is obliged to secure every one's property." To give laws, to receive obedience, to compel with the sword, belong to none but the civil magistrate, and on this ground we affirm that the magistrate's power extends not to the establishing any articles of faith or forms of worship, by force of laws; for laws are of no force without penalties. The care of souls cannot belong to the civil magistrate, because his power consists only in outward force; but pure and saving religion consists in the inward persuasion of the mind, without which nothing can be acceptable to God.

It is a just position, and cannot be too firmly established, that we can have no property in that which another may take, when he pleases, to himself, neither can we have the proper enjoyment of our religious liberties, (which must be acknowledged to be of greater,) if held by the same unjust and capricious tenure; and this must appear to be the case when temporary laws pretend to grant relief so very inadequate.

It may now be asked—*What is the liberty desired?* The answer is, as the kingdom of Christ is not of this world, and religion is a concern between God and the soul, with which no human authority can intermeddle, consistently with the principles of Christianity, and according to the dictates of Protestantism, we claim and expect the liberty of worshipping God according to our consciences, not being obliged to support a ministry we cannot attend, whilst we demean ourselves as faithful subjects. These we have an undoubted right to, as men, as Christians, and by charter as inhabitants of Massachusetts Bay.

The conduct of the Massachusetts delegates at this conference was not very friendly to the Baptists, so much were their minds warped by the religious tyrannies complained of. The truth is, these delegates, subsequently known among the great statesmen of our country, did not yet grasp the full idea of liberty of conscience for which Baptists then, as ever, were pleading. Their minds only comprehended liberty as freedom from the domination of the British Throne. They did not rise to the great height for which Baptists were aiming, viz.: Soul Liberty. It is not in a spirit of egotism, but that of utmost candor, when we affirm, that to this stand under God, taken by the Baptists, the people of this country owe their *Religious* Liberty, more than to any other influence. How far prejudice will carry even good men, however, will be indicated by John Adams' account of the above conference in Carpenter's Hall. It is as follows:—

"Governor Hopkins and Governor Ward, of Rhode Island, came to our lodgings and said to us that President Manning, of Rhode Island

College, and Mr. Backus, of Massachusetts, were in town, and had conversed with some gentlemen in Philadelphia, and wished we would meet them at six in the evening, at Carpenter's Hall. Whether they explained their designs more particularly to any of my colleagues I know not, but I had no idea of the design. We all went at the hour, and, to my great surprise, found the hall almost full of people, and a great number of Quakers seated at the long table, with their broad-brimmed beavers on their heads. We were invited to seats among them, and informed that they had received complaints from some Anabaptists and some Friends in Massachusetts, against certain laws of that province restrictive of the liberty of conscience, and some instances were mentioned in the general court and in the courts of justice in which Friends and Anabaptists had been grievously oppressed. I know not how my colleagues felt, being, like my friend Chase, naturally quick and warm, at seeing our state and her delegates thus summoned before a self-created tribunal, which was neither legal nor constitutional.

"Israel Pemberton, a Quaker, of large property and more intrigue, began to speak, and said that Congress were here endeavouring to form a union of the colonies; but there were difficulties in the way, and none of more importance than liberty of conscience. The laws of New England, and particularly of Massachusetts, were inconsistent with it, for they not only compelled men to pay to the building of churches and support ministers, but to some known religious assembly on first days, etc.; and that he and his friends were desirous of engaging us to assure them that our state would repeal all those laws and place things as they are in Pennsylvania.

A suspicion instantly arose in my mind, which I have ever believed to have been well founded, that this artful Jesuit, for I had been apprised before of his character, was endeavoring to avail himself of this opportunity to break up the Congress or, at least, withdraw the Quakers and the governing part of Pennsylvania from us; for, at that time, by means of a most unequal representation, the Quakers had a majority in the House of Assembly, and, by consequence, the whole power of the state in their hands. I arose and spoke in answer to him. The substance of what I said was, that we had no authority to bind our constituents to any such proposals; that the laws of Massachusetts were of the most mild and equitable establishment; that it would be in vain for us to enter into any conference on such a subject, for we knew beforehand our constituents would disavow all we could do or say for the satisfaction of those who invited us to this meeting. That the people of Massachusetts were as religious and consciencious as the people of Pennsylvania; that their conscience dictated to them that it was their duty to support those laws, and, therefore, that very liberty of conscience which Mr. Pemberton invoked would demand indulgence for the tender consciences of the people of Massachusetts, and allow them to preserve their laws; that it might be depended on this was a point that could not be carried; that I would deceive them by insinuating the faintest hope, for I knew they might as well turn the heavenly bodies out of their annual and diurnal courses as the people of Massachusetts at the present day from their meeting-house and Sunday laws. Pemberton made no reply but this, ' Oh, sir, pray don't urge liberty of conscience in favor of such laws.' If I had but known the particular complaints which were to have been alleged, and if Pemberton had not broken irregularly into the midst of things, it might have been better, perhaps to have postponed this declaration. However, the gentleman proceeded and stated the particular cases of oppression which were alleged in our general and executive courts. It happened that Mr. Cushing and Mr. Samuel Adams had been present in the general court when the petitions had been under deliberation, and they explained the whole so clearly that every reasonable man must have been satisfied. Mr. Paine and I had been concerned at the bar in every action in the executive courts which was complained of, and we explained them all to the entire satisfaction of impartial men, and showed that there had been no oppression or injustice in any of them. In his diary, Mr. Adams describes the affair thus, "In the evening we were invited to an interview at Carpenter's Hall, with the Quakers and Anabaptists. Mr. Backus is come here from Middleborough with a design to apply to the Congress for a redress of grievances of the anti-pedo-baptists in our Province. The cases from Chelmsford, the case of Mr. White. of Haverhill, the case of Ashfield and Warwick were mentioned by Mr. Backus. Old Israel Pemberton was quite rude, and his rudeness was resented; but the conference, which held till eleven o'clock, I hope will produce good."

The evening succeeding the above conference, the committee appointed by the Philadelphia Association held a meeting, and in the account of their proceedings say, "We think it did appear that the delegates from Boston were determined to support the claim the Legislature made to a right to make penal laws in matters of religion." It was further resolved, " That the committee, not being satisfied with the declaration made last evening by the delegates from Massachusetts Bay, are determined to pursue every prudent measure to obtain a full and complete redress for all grievances, for our brethren in New England."

Arrangements were also made to supply each of the

delegates with a copy of the Memorial read by Dr. Manning, a copy of the above resolution and a copy of Dr. Backus' "Appeal to the Public." These documents and the conduct of the "Committee on Grievances" exerted a powerful influence in the direction desired, even though the course pursued and the object desired by the brethren from New England was grossly misrepresented by the dominant church party in that quarter as well as by the Delegates in Congress from Boston and vicinity.

Meetings for fasting and prayer were now held in the churches of the Philadelphia Association four times a year, and the men yearned in soul for entire liberty of conscience as much as for freedom from the increasing tyrannies of Great Britain. At the Association, in 1775, Rev. Samuel Stillman was present, and was probably supplying the pulpit of the First Church. His name is given in the minutes as though he was actually pastor of the Church. Rev. William Rogers resigned the pastorate in March, but continued to supply the pulpit until the following June, in conjunction with Thomas Fleeson, a licentiate of the Church.

CHAPTER XII.—1776-1780.

THE EVER MEMORABLE 1776.—DECLARATION OF INDEPENDENCE.—ASSOCIATION AT SCOTCH PLAINS.—DAYS OF HUMILIATION.—INDEPENDENCE HALL.—BAPTISTS ON THE SIDE OF THE COLONIES.—REV. WILLIAM ROGERS A CHAPLAIN.—INGENUITY OF BURGIS ALLISON.—REV. JOHN PITMAN.—PATRIOTISM OF THE PENNYPACK CHURCH.—NO ASSOCIATION IN 1777.—PHILADELPHIA CHURCH IN DISTRESS.—REV. JAMES MANNING.—DIARY OF MANNING IN PHILADELPHIA.—PRICE OF BOARD.—LETTER TO REVS. STILL AND MILLER.—REV. JOHN GANO CALLED.—WINDOWS FILLED WITH BOARDS.—GANO'S REPLY.—CALL REPEATED.—ELHANAN WINCHESTER CHOSEN.—AN UNFORTUNATE MOVE.—REV. DAVID JONES.—FIRST HUNDRED YEARS.

WE now reach the ever memorable year of 1776, during which, on the Fourth of July, the Declaration of American Independence was adopted in Independence Hall. How much the Baptists had to do with bringing about the passage of that glorious instrument and its grand results, Dr. William Cathcart, of this city, has ably shown in his work, entitled, "The Baptists and the American Revolution."

The Philadelphia Association was to have been held, this year, in New York, but owing to the troubles in the country, a more retired place was selected; hence it met at Scotch Plains, New Jersey. That year the membership of the four churches in the city and county of Philadelphia amounted to 361. The following is from the minutes of 1776 :—

This Association, taking into consideration the awful impending calamities of these times, and deeply impressed with a sense of our duty to humble ourselves before God, by acknowledging our manifold sins, and imploring his pardon and interposition in favor of our distressed country; and also to beseech Him to grant that such blessings may accompany the means of His grace that a revival of pure and undefiled religion may universally prevail:

Resolved, That it be, and is hereby recommended to our churches,

INDEPENDENCE HALL.

INDEPENDENCE HALL, AS IT APPEARED IN 1776.

to observe four days of humiliation in the year ensuing, by prayer, abstinence from food, and labor, and recreations, lawful on other days. The days proposed for humiliation, are the Fridays before the last Lord's day in November, February, May and August.

Our denomination in these parts took the side of the Colonies against the Mother Country, and there are on record many illustrations of their patriotism and loyalty. In March, 1776, the General Assembly of Pennsylvania voted to organize three battalions of foot, for the defence of the Province, and appointed Rev. William Rogers, late pastor of the First Church, to be the sole Chaplain of the said forces. "In June, 1778, he was promoted to a Brigade Chaplaincy in the Continental Army, which office he continued to hold till June, 1781, when he retired from military service altogether."

Burgis Allison, a licentiate of the Pennypack Church, when the British were in possession of Philadelphia, exerted his ingenuity, as well as manifested his patriotism, by preparing kegs containing explosive substances, which were floated down the Delaware river for the destruction of the British men-of-war, lying at anchor near this city.

After the passage of the "Boston Port Bill," in 1774, John Pitman moved from that city, where he was a member of the First Baptist Church, to Philadelphia, and became a member of one of the Baptist churches here. During three years he was engaged in secular business, but in 1776 he joined a volunteer company, consisting principally of Quakers, and thereafter, with Christian firmness, patriotism and piety, he was identified with the colonists. As early as 1777 we find him preaching the gospel in various parts of New Jersey, and on October 12, 1777, he became pastor at Upper Freehold. July 30, 1778, there is a record in the minutes of the Pennypack Church which is significant of that church's patriotism. It is as follows:—

Elizabeth Foster suspended until she shall clear herself of the charge of sending the English army, or a detachment of it, to plunder Captain Lanehlen.

In 1777 there was no meeting of the Association, in consequence of the ravages of war, and Philadelphia being occupied by the British troops. In 1778 it was held at Hopewell, N. J., and for the next five successive years at Philadelphia. After 1776, until 1781, no statistics of the churches are given in the minutes of the Association. The meetings were characterized by a devotional spirit rather than that of business. All felt the depressing circumstances of the country.

What was the exact condition of the church in Philadelphia from May 8, 1775, to August 16, 1779, is very difficult to determine, as there are no church minutes extant of that period. It was owing to the war, the absence of many members in the army, the high prices of all the necessaries of life, and the long occupation of the city by the British army. At the latter date we find Rev. James Manning, of Rhode Island, with them. He had come to Philadelphia to learn about the financial plans of Congress, with special reference to the interests of Brown University, and finding the Baptist church in such a sad condition, he devoted some three weeks to their interests. Between Providence and Philadelphia he visited many churches. His wife accompanied him on this visit. The account of this trip is given in his diary very minutely, relative to Philadelphia. From Guild's Memoir of him we quote the following, which will be in place:—

Monday, June 28. Set out and travelled [from Southampton] to Pennypack, Mr. Jones', [Rev. Samuel Jones]. Arrived in the evening, and found the family well and glad to see us. Tarried here until July 2 ; spent the time agreeably in viewing the farm, its products, harvests, etc., and in conversation. The season here extremely hot ; height of wheat harvest ; the grain struck with the red rust, though little injured, except the rye, which is much blasted. The greatest part of the harvest between here and Philadelphia, where we arrived at eleven o'clock A. M., July 2, is gathered. Put up at Mr. Goforth's, [a member of the Baptist church] and my horse across the way, in Second street, between Race and Vine streets. Visited Samuel Davis, [Deacon of the church] but he was out of town; also Mr. Rogers. Called at Mr. Watkins' [formerly a deacon of the church]; then at Mr. Wescott's [a deacon of the church]; from thence to Dr. Rush's [one of the signers of the Declaration of Independence], who treated me politely; from thence called on Messrs. Shields and Moulder [Baptists]. Called at Mr. Hart's lodgings, but he was out, which was also the case at Mr. Robert Jones'. The evening of July 2, Mr. Joseph Hart, of the Executive Council, spent at my lodgings.

Saturday, July 3. This morning came out a paper, in which Congress was handled pretty severely, under the signature of Leonidas. Breakfasted at Dr. Rush's, and received two hundred dollars, Dr. Finley's draft on him. Spent the afternoon chiefly in writing to Providence, by Mr. Ellery, who sets off this afternoon. Went to the State House; met Mr. Collins, and inquired, without much satisfaction, what was on foot in Congress, relative to money. Dined at Mr. Redwood's with Mr. Ellery, and returned to my lodgings, where were Messrs. Shields and Connolly, who spent the afternoon with us.

Lord's Day, July 4. Preached twice with some freedom; the morning congregation thin; more in the afternoon. Both church and society here in a broken state. The people urgent for my tarrying a considerable time, which did not suit my affairs. In the evening I visited one of the members of the church near her end; appeared to be in a happy frame of mind Attended a religious society composed of Baptists, Presbyterians and church people. They appeared very serious and somewhat engaged in religion. Found Gen. Spencer at my lodgings, now a member of Congress. It being Fourth of July, the anniversary of Independence, the Chaplains of Congress preached suitable to the occasion, and Congress attended. High mass was celebrated and Te Deum sung at the Romish chapel. The gentlemen of the town were invited by billets, from the French minister, to attend. I suppose these causes rendered the Baptist meetings thinner than otherwise. The lowering of prices by the committee is considered by the town as a violent measure and only a temporary relief, but think it will share the fate of former state bills. The suburbs of this city greatly destroyed by the English, but the body of it not much damaged. A fine rain on the night of the Fourth. Some more apples in these parts than in the Jerseys.

Monday, July 5. Breakfasted at Mr. Shields, where a committee from the church met and importuned me to tarry with them some time, or come again and make them a longer visit. I gave them hopes of the latter after the four Sabbaths of this month. Went to Mr. David Bower's, and thence to Mr. Moulder's; then to hear the oration at the Dutch church; the performance indifferent, Congress and the French Ambassador present, and a large assembly. Here met Mr. Merchant and called at his lodgings. Received an invitation to dine at Prof. Lawren's, but we dined at Mr. Wescott's. Returned to our lodgings. Were visted by Messrs. Shields, Britain, and Gen. Spencer. Set out in the afternoon for Mr. Jones' [Rev. Samuel Jones], where we arrived in the evening. The weather intensely hot.

Tuesday, July 6. Tarried at Mr. Jones', and set out on the 7th for Bordentown.

The above record indicates a busy nine days in Philadelphia. On Tuesday, the 27th, he again reached Rev. Samuel Jones', and on the 29th came into the city. We quote again from his diary:—

Put up my horse at Mr. Shields', called on some friends, and took quarters at Mr. Samuel Davis'.

Friday, July 30. Visited some friends in town.

Saturday, 31st. Saw the British prisoners taken at Stony Point, march in; fine looking men. Dined at Mr Goforth's.

Sunday, August 1st. Preached twice. The congregation pretty large—more so than usual here,—and very attentive. Spent the evening at a religious conference, where there seemed a degree of of quickening and freedom.

August 2nd. A storm of rain from the northeast, which continued the next day; heat intense. I tarried mostly at my lodgings.

August 4th. Wrote letters to Providence, to the church and Nicholas Brown.

August 5th. The account of the defeat of the British by the French fleet in the West Indies arrived. Spent the evening at Major Goforth's, in company with several gentlemen. Here I met Major Somner, ten days from Providence, who tells me that things are agreeable in that quarter. which I was also informed of by a letter from General Varnum, received yesterday. G. Brigade is come to headquarters, which I heard by a line from Van Horn, at the same time.

Friday 6th. Delivered my letters to Mr. Somner. This day Mr. Edwards called upon me, and tarried in town several days. Saw General Spencer and Mr. Collins. Abundance of rumors concerning the West India affair. Visited in town in the forenoon.

Saturday 7th. Went with Mr. Edwards to Captain Falkner's, five miles, and spent the afternoon agreeably.

Sunday, August 8th. Preached three times. The assembly full, and the people so importunate for another Sabbath that I concluded to stay.

Monday, August 9th. Messrs. Jones, Blackwell, and Nathaniel Stout came to town; the former tarried with me one night.

Tuesday, August 10th. Mr. Edwards, in company with Jones and myself, set out for Colonel Miles. Distance thirteen miles. Arrived in the evening, and he and lady next morning, from town. He has a most elegant seat, gardens, meadows, etc., and a most remarkable spring, which turns three wheels in one fourth of a mile from its source. Spent three days very agreeably, and on the 13th, set out for town, Mr. Edwards returning with Mr. Jones. The weather extremely hot, and abundance of rain. The Indian corn incomparably fine, the buckwheat forward, and the second crop of grass cutting. This is an agreeable part of the country. Preached this evening.

Saturday, August 14th. Visited Major Goforth's, paid my barber; received one hundred dollars of Mr. Rogers, as per order; called at Mr. Morris' and dined at Mr. Ball's.

Sunday, August 15th. Extremely hot. Preached twice, attended the funeral of a child, and drank chocolate at Mr. Turner's. Richard Lemon and both the McKims, from Baltimore, at meeting.

Monday, August 16th. Visited Mr. Moulders, and attended the meeting of the church and society, who unanimously agreed to get the pulpit supplied. Chose a committee of eight, half from the church and half from the society, to raise the necessary supplies for that purpose, and to call Mr. Gano for one year. At two o'clock set out for Mr. Jones. Preached at Pennepek at five o'clock. Tarried with Mr. Jones and Mr. Edwards. The weather intensely hot; though the season uncommonly wet.

Tuesday, August 17th. Set out for Bordentown.

During the stay of Rev. James Manning in this city, he aided very materially in gathering together the scattered forces of the Baptist Church, and in preparing the way for the regular ministry of the word amongst them again. As an illustration of the price of living here then, the church paid fifty dollars a week for his board. The following letter addressed to Rev. Messrs. Still and Miller, will indicate the feelings of and throw some light upon the trials through which the church had passed during those fearful years:—

Sir, we need not inform you that we have been for a long time as sheep having no shepherd, and the consequence has been that we have strayed one from another. But your late visit amongst us seemed to cause some shaking among the dry bones, and could you have stayed longer, doubt not but the divine flame would have become more universal. And we can with pleasure inform you that, during Mr. Manning's stay amongst us, the church and congregation were considerably collected together, and there appeared more love and unity than we have seen for some time past, which is a matter of encouragement to us, to use our best endeavours to have the pulpit supplied in future. Before Mr. Manning left us the church and congregation were called together to consult on ways and means for supplying the pulpit, till we can get a minister to settle amongst us. At which time a committee was chosen, and a subscription opened to enable the committee to defray the expenses of supplies. Therefore in the name and behalf of the church and congregation we their committee earnestly solicit you to visit us as soon as you possibly can, that a vacancy may be prevented, and if you and Mr. Miller could supply us till the Association, we believe it would be agreeable to all, and would willingly flatter ourselves, that you would have reason to say at the close that it was good for you that you came amongst us. And as you minister to us in spiritual, we hope our hearts will be enlarged so as to minister to you of our temporal things. We mean to provide lodgings, and use our best endeavors to make you comfortable during your stay with us. We hope therefore you will take the matter into your serious consideration, and that God may influence you in our favor is and shall be the prayer of your brethren in the Gospel.

Philadelphia, Aug. 25th, 1779. Signed, { GEORGE WESCOTT, SAMUEL DAVIS.

In 1778, an invitation was extended to Rev. John Gano, a brother in law of Rev. James Manning, to settle as their pastor, but the condition and prospects of the field were so uninviting that he declined. In September, 1779, another very long and earnest letter was written to him, entreating him by every consideration to come and settle with them. Two copies of this letter were sent, one to his family in New Jersey and the other to the army, as it was uncertain just where he was at the time. As to the straits to which the church was put about this time may be learned from the following Minute dated November 6, 1779:—

Joseph Watkins is desired to get the broken panes of the Baptist Church filled up with boards.

Rev. John Gano replied at length to the call of the church, which he was compelled to decline. His letter, considering all its contents and the time at which it was written, is a valuable historical document and throws some light upon the trials then endured even by the men prominent in the Christian ministry. Mr. Gano was an able divine, a true patriot, a fine specimen of a Christian man, and loyal to the great principles of the Baptist denomination. The letter was penned in Philadelphia, as follows :—

I have received your call, have considered its contents, for and sympathize with you and the cause you are pained for the promotion of in this place. I thank you for the respect expressed therein, and think the more of it as you have long known me. Nineteen years ago I served this church steadily for a season, my defects and the expenses of my family were then known and borne with, the time being expired, and your expected supply coming from abroad, you had no further need of my services. Then I accepted a call to New York. Christian friendship has continued. Yet suffer me now to remark without feigned humility, I was then in my own esteem unequal to the place, although then in the prime, now in the decline of life, my family then small, now large and more expensive; the church, probably from its late political difficulties, the death and removal of members, the heavy taxes of the times, may be less able to bear the charge of a family like mine, who having been long unsettled, and flying from place to place, which, with losses and expenses, without the advantage of replacing, are reduced to an appearance however neighborly like, in a back place, yet rather reproachful in this place, to a church like this. Neither is the sum mentioned in your call at the present exchange anyway adequate to a present support, all which I could leave to God, did I satisfactorily know his will and consequently my duty in the present case. I do not. I am obliged to compare my present standing in the army, the mere Providence that put and has preserved me there, the ways and means of a former and a present support for my family, with this call to learn my duty. And that you may be better judges with me, I must be explicit in stating the contrast in my own breast as I in some measure sensibly feel it at present. I have said providence put and has continued me in the army for these reasons— I never sought it, neither did I expect to like the life. Many things I have and must see and hear in the army very abhorrent, but little christian conversation, no retirement for study, discouraging prospects for convening or converting sinners, or quickening and edifying God's children, and having no disposition to court the hardships and fatigues of campaigning, and had not the contest appeared to me just, and of so much importance to my country, both in a civil and religious sense, as to render me incapable of refusing any services or suffering I might be called to in it, at the same time knowing there were popular men of character in the ministry that left the city also, and some in the State beside, that by their temporary acceptance manifested a readiness to the service, that on the whole I have not known but God meant to keep me ready as an instrument in some future, when the enemy shall leave New York city, to assist that broken church where so much of the best of my time has been spent (and leave it they will, or come here again), and should I leave the army contrary to the desire of not only those of the first military characters in the State as also some eminent in the civil, I should probably in a late day fling all those advantages that I might expect from the state in favor of that church into a hand not so amical to it. My family has somehow been preserved and supported, neither is the prospect at present less promising for the future. We late last Spring got on a little place, although much out of repairs, and a poor habitation, it is fertile in pasturage and will afford near twenty tons of hay, has an orchard, and my son, although an entire stranger to farming, yet turned in to assist the family, and with a little help they procured and raised something of a summer crop of almost every kind, and has now near twenty acres of wheat in the ground, which place I rent at sixty-seven pounds continental per year—many disadvantages we are under and particularly the education of children. This view of the case I hope will show you my difficulty in determining, and I expect you will not take it unkind should I not accept your invitation.

The call was repeated over and over again. Every effort was made to secure him, but of no avail. He felt it to be his duty to remain as Chaplain in the army, and did so until the war closed.

Mr. Gano, in his autobiography, published in 1806, thus briefly refers to this event :

I obtained a furlough, to visit and tarry some time with my family. While here I received a letter from the Baptist church in Philadelphia, requesting me to come and supply them. I shewed the letter to General Clinton, who gave me leave to pay them a visit for two or three weeks. I informed the church that I was not discharged from the army, neither did I wish to engage myself to any people. For if, in the providence of God, the enemy should be driven from New York, I intend to collect my scattered church, and to settle myself in that place. I therefore wished them to look for a supply elsewhere.

While in Philadelphia he was taken very ill, which detained him from the army for some time.

In 1775 the church, after the resignation of Rev. William Rodgers, endeavored to get Rev. Elhanan Winchester, but without success. October 23, 1780, however, "the church made choice of Mr. Winchester to be their minister." He was born in Brookline, Mass., September 30, 1751, and united with a church there about 1770. Subsequently his views on baptism changed, and in 1771 he was baptized by Rev. Ebenezer Lyon, and became a member of the Baptist church at Canterbury, Ct. He at once entered upon the work of the ministry and preached for a time at Rehoboth, Mass., then in different parts of New England and South Carolina. He was zealous, eloquent and a man of remarkable memory. Great success attended his preaching, crowds assembled to hear him, and he was in demand by the churches. These elements of character had their influence on the church in Philadelphia, but his settlement was one of the most unfortunate moves they ever made, as the sequel will show.

Rev. John Gano, in his letter to the First Baptist Church, as given in this chapter, speaks of "popular men of character in the ministry that left the city, and some in the state," to enter the chaplaincy of the country. One of these men certainly merits reference here, not that he was a Philadelphia Baptist, but as the ancestor of an honored family of our denomination in this city. Rev. David Jones is the gentleman spoken of. He was born in Delaware, May 12, 1736, and baptized at the Welsh Tract Church, May 6, 1758. After a liberal course of study he entered the ministry, and was ordained at Freehold, New Jersey, December 12th, 1766. Previous to the issuing of the Declaration of Independence he took high ground in favor of cutting loose from Great Britian. In 1776 he became a chaplain in the army, and remained through all the war, up to the surrender at Yorktown, performing very important services for his country. He was a man of warm friendship, ardent patriotism and sincere piety, and, after much faithful work for his Lord and Master, he died February 5th, 1824, in the 84th year of his age. He was buried in the graveyard of the Great Valley Baptist Church, near to the very spot where, for many years, as a pastor, he preached the gospel of the blessed God.

With this decade we conclude the first century of the history of Philadelphia Baptists. The first hundred years were checkered and trying. The progress was slow, but with the blessing of God upon the humble endeavors of his people about seven hundred persons were added to their fellowship by baptism, and from the little Baptist colony of 1684 the number had grown, by 1780, notwithstanding the ravages of war, to 224, having three well established and highly respected and respectable churches. About fifteen different men had served the churches in the ministry, while others had been raised up and sent forth to various parts of our country. Brown University had been founded, and a good basis laid for future work and success.

CHAPTER XIII.—1781-1782.

APOSTACY OF WINCHESTER.—PROTEST.—COUNCIL CALLED.—ADVICE OF ASSOCIATION.—LAWSUIT FOR PROPERTY.—EXCOMMUNICATED.—ADDRESS FROM THE CHURCH.—WINCHESTER'S DEATH.—BAPTISTERION. – REV. JAMES MANNING'S LETTER.—ISSUES OF THE WAR. —MESSENGER FROM YORKTOWN.—ASSOCIATION IN SESSION.—MET AT SUNRISE.—SUCCESS OF AMERICAN ARMS.—STATISTICS OF CHURCHES.—OUT OF THE ORDEAL.—PETITION THE GENERAL ASSEMBLY.—ASK TO BE INCORPORATED.—DESIRE PRESIDENT MANNING.—REV. THOMAS USTICK SETTLED.—SKETCH OF USTICK.—CIRCULATION OF THE BIBLE.—BROWN UNIVERSITY COMMENDED.—HONEYWELL SCHOOL FUND.—JOHN HONEYWELL'S WILL.

THE very beginning of this decade was clouded with the apostacy of Elhanan Winchester, pastor of the church in Philadelphia. The first reference to it in the records is under date of Monday, March 5, 1781, as follows :—

It being mentioned in the church that Mr. Winchester held the doctrine of of universal restoration, much debating ensued in consequence thereof, when, finding nothing satisfactory could be done, and growing late, the following protest was entered down to be signed by those who meant to preserve the orthodox faith, viz. : " Whereas the doctrine of universal restoration of bad men and angels, in the fullest extent, has for a considerable time privately, and of late more publicly, been introduced among us, and is now openly avowed by some of the members, to the great disorder and confusion of our church, and wounding the hearts of many of our brethren contrary to our confession of faith, we, whose names are underwritten, do in the most solemn manner, from a real conviction of duty, seriously protest against the same as a *most dangerous heresy:*

WILLIAM ROGERS, Samuel Miles, John McKim, Thomas Shields, Joseph Watkins, Benjamin Shaw, John Levering, Anthony Levering, Philip Burgen, Isaac Powell, George Ingles, William Moore, John McCleod, William Harper, David Bowen, Abraham Mitchell, Matthias Mavis, Isaac Bellangee, James Hunter, Abraham Levering, Jacob Levering, Andrew Edge, Jacob Burkeloe, Enoch Morgan, John Flintham, William Hungary, Ezekiel Robins, Richard Riley, Christian Dick, William Jenkins, John Bazelee, Zebediah David. MORGAN EDWARDS signs this protest against the doctrine of universal salvation under the character only of a doctrine that he does not believe. Martha Scott, Abigail Aiger, Mary Rush, Ann Barnes, Frances G. Mitchell, Elizabeth Ellison, Sarah Powell, Ann Wilson, Sarah Sutton, Hannah Rush, Elizabeth Burgen, Ann Faries, Sarah Moulder, Mary Bright, Sarah Marsh, Elizabeth Bazelee, Martha Davis, Elizabeth Rees, Jane Nicholson, Mary Siddons, Fanny Old, Sarah Connell, Mary Hammitt, Ann Mackan, Margaret McNilleans, Sarah Gardiner, Catharine Rensord, Mary Parker, Lydia Shields, Elizabeth Ball, Rachael Davis, Sarah Davis, Eleanor Kessler, Mary Dungan, Mary Holget, Sarah Edge, Hannah Levering, Anna Levering, Margaret Wilson, Elizabeth Brockis, Sarah Taylor, Elizabeth Marsh, Elizabeth Marot, Martha Burkeloe, Margaret Erwin, Rachael Wilson, Massey Engles, Elizabeth Winebridge, Margaret Conner, Mary Paine, Sarah Tricketts, Rebecca Lakur, Rachael Test, Martha Coffin, Catherine Standland, Sarah Parsons, Hester Davis, Lydia Gilbert, Hannah Rogers. Total 92.

Mr. Winchester was requested to desist from supplying the pulpit. Much trouble ensued; church meetings were frequent; a council of ministers was called, but their advice was disregarded by the Winchester party, which party broke open the church and held services there. Thus matters continued for a whole year. The Council of Ministers decided that those who adhered to the Confession of Faith and against Winchester were the church. The matter was carried to the Association in 1781. The committee appointed by that body to consider the subject reported as follows :—

First. That the proceedings of the protesters in that business were regular and fair. Secondly. That the declaration of the ministers who were called to their assistance respecting the protestors, was weighty, full and decisive. Thirdly. That, although the non-signers are virtually excluded, yet, in order to their more formal excommunication, the Philadelphia Church be advised to appoint at their meeting of business two of their regular male members to go with the protest to the non-protestors, one by one, in order to their signing it, and warn them that in case they refuse to sign, should openly and formally, by name, be excommunicated.

SAMUEL JONES,
OLIVER HART, } *Committee.*
ABEL MORGAN,
JAMES MANNING,

The Association, "*Resolved* unanimously, That the above report of the committee is approved; and that this Association advise all the churches to beware of Elhanan Winchester, and not admit him, or any who advocate 'universal salvation,' to the offices of public teaching, or suffer any who avow the same to continue in their communion."

Winchester and his party sought to get possession of the property by lawsuit, which added to the trouble and expense. In this he failed, for on July 9, 1784, after a two days' trial, the jury decided against him. All attempts at reconciliation were useless, and the church in December excommunicated, publicly, forty-six persons for adhering to the doctrine of Universalism. Some of these subsequently saw their error, sought restoration to the fellowship of the church, and maintained until death fealty to the doctrines and ordinances of the New Testament. About fifty pages of the church records are taken up with the proceedings relative to this case, but it is unnecessary to quote from them, as we have given the main facts. By the authority of the church a pamphlet of sixteen pages was published, entitled, "An Address from the Baptist Church in Philadelphia to their sister Churches of the same denomination throughout the Confederate States of North America. Drawn up by a Committee of the Church, appointed for said purpose." It was printed in this city, in 1781, by Robert Aitken. This little book rehearses the troubles with Winchester, but it is not necessary to quote from it further than to say that he came to Philadelphia in October 1780, "as a messenger from the Warren Association to ours, which was nigh at hand. Many of the members having, previous to this repeatedly heard him preach, not the least suspicion existed but that he continued an advocate for that faith which we look upon as the *faith once delivered to the saints.*" After his exclusion from the Baptist denomination he continued to preach for some years in Philadelphia to his adherents. In 1787 he went to London. His death occurred April 18, 1797, when he was forty-six years of age.

Early 1782, a lot was purchased by the First Church, on the Schuylkill river, at the end of Spruce Street, to afford facilities for baptism to be administered. For many years the place was known as "The Baptisterion." Morgan Edwards thus describes it as he saw it shortly after his arrival in this country:—

Around said spot are large oaks affording fine shade—underfoot is a green, variegated with wild flowers and aromatic herbs, and a tasteful house is near for dressing and undressing the candidates.

Watson in his "Annals of Philadelphia," says:—

In the midst of the spot was a large stone, upon the dry ground, and elevated above it about three feet, made level on the top by art, with hewn steps to ascend to it. Around this rock the candidates knelt to pray, and upon it the preacher stood to preach to the people. I have learned that the property there belonged to Mr. Marsh, a Baptist, and that the British army cut down the trees for fuel. The whole place is now all wharfed out for the coal trade. The "Stone of Witness" is buried in the wharf, never to be seen more.

The spot remained bare of trees after they had been destroyed by the British army, in the Revolution, for nearly a a quarter of a century. In a letter written August 3rd, 1784, to Rev. John Ryland, of London, by Rev. James Manning, he thus referred to the Winchester trouble:—

The apostacy of Mr. Winchester has been for a lamentation amongst us. Self-exaltation was the rock on which he split. Though he had from the first been remarkable for instability of character, he inflicted a grievous wound on the cause, especially in Philadelphia, but I think he is now at the end of his tether. His interest is declining, which will most probably prove a dead wound. I saw him last May, and from his appearance think he has nearly run his race. His state of health will not admit of his preaching, and by a letter last week from the Rev. Thomas Ustick, who now supplies the pulpit in Philadelphia, I learn that Winchester and his friends have lost the case in their suit for the meeting-house and the property of the church. It really appeared that God owned his labors in the revival in New England; perhaps for attempting to take the glory to himself, he has laid him aside as an improper instrument for his work, who justly challenges the whole of it as his own. From common fame, and from what I myself saw, I really think this to be the case.

Amidst all the excitement incident to this case there was still the deepest solicitude felt for the successful issues of the war. This anxiety was duly rewarded on October 19th, 1781, when Cornwallis surrendered the posts at Yorktown and Gloucester into the hands of Washington. This was in reality the final blow to the British power in this country. A messenger, with a despatch from Gen. Washington, reached Philadelphia on Tuesday the 23rd, at midnight, bearing the news of the surrender. Before the dawn of Wednesday the exulting people filled the streets, and at an early hour the cheering letter was read to Congress, and that body thereupon went in procession to church, and there joined in devout thanksgiving to God for the great victory. The Philadelphia Baptist Association was then in session; and while it had been saddened by the defection of Elhanan Winchester, whose troubles were considered the very day there was so much exultation over the news from Yorktown, it was made joyous beyond expression by the victory which had been achieved, under God, by the American arms. No wonder, therefore, that on Thursday the Association "*Met at Sunrise.*" The conclusion of the session is thus recorded in the Minutes :—

> And now, dear brethren, having come to a close of our annual meeting, before we address you by our circular letter, we feel ourselves constrained to acknowledge the great goodness of God towards us, and to call on you to join with us in thankfulness and praise, as well for the unanimity and brotherly love which prevailed throughout our meeting, as for the recent signal success granted to the American arms, in the surrender of the whole British army, under the command of Lord Cornwallis, with the effusion of so little blood.

After an omission of four years the statistics of the

churches are again given this year, showing a membership at Pennypack of fifty-eight and at Philadelphia of eighty-six. There was no intelligence from Montgomery, whose membership was about eighty. In all the dark days of the past six years, the churches had suffered fearfully, and the one in Philadelphia had her share. It was indeed very trying that, after the sorrows and sacrifices of the war, this body should be torn, as it was, by the enunciation of false doctrine on the part of a trusted leader. Yet, like gold tried in the fire, she came out of the ordeal purified and prepared to begin afresh for God and truth.

A committee was appointed by the church May 7th, 1781, consisting of five persons "to prepare a petition to lay before the General Assembly of this State, setting forth our present and much injured situation, by Elhanan Winchester and his adherents, and pray them to take our case immediately into their consideration and yield us the necessary redress by putting us in quiet possession of our meeting-house and all the proprety appertaining to the Baptist Church in this city—and also *that they will incorporate us as a Church.*"

In October, 1781, the church tried hard to induce President Manning, of Brown University, who had come on to attend the Philadelphia Association, to settle with them, but he declined, thanking them very kindly for their friendly opinion of him. He, however, recommended Thomas Ustick as a person every way qualified to suit them, except "that he had a large and rising family, and would expect that they should be provided for." On the 29th a letter was accordingly sent to him, requesting very urgently a visit with a view to settlement. He complied, and spent the winter with them, with great acceptance. March 4, 1782, they called him to supply them for one year, which he accepted, and removed with his family to Philadelphia in July, bearing a letter of commendation for himself and wife from the First Baptist Church in Providence, R. I., dated June 16, 1782. His was a difficult position to fill, coming, as he did, right after the trouble with Winchester, who had established in the vicinity another congregation, where he preached universal salvation with considerable effect; added to all this was the long and trying war through which the country had passed. Nevertheless, he was equal to the task, and, under his ministry, the church began to assume her former prosperity. At the end of the first year he was requested to continue his labors, and on January 5th, 1784, with his wife, was received into the fellowship of the church. Mr. Ustick was born in the city of New York, August 30, 1735. At the the age of thirteen, in his native city, he was baptized on the profession of his faith, by Rev. John Gano. Mr. Gano, ever apt on such occasions, in giving out the hymn to be sung, so changed it that it read,

"His honor is engaged to save
The *youngest* of his sheep."

In the simplicity of his childlike nature, young Ustick, as he walked down into the water with his pastor, asked, "Why did you not read the word as it is, "the *meanest* of his sheep; for so, truly, I am?"

It very frequently occurs that one whom the Lord calls so early into His fold, He subsequently calls to the work of preaching the gospel. It was so with Thomas Ustick, and he began almost at once after his conversion to prosecute a course of study under Rev. James Manning, at Warren and Providence, R. I. He graduated from Brown University September 4, 1771, at the age of nineteen years. At first he became a teacher of a school, but continued his studies with a view to the ministry. In 1774 he received the degree of Master of Arts, and was licensed to preach about the same time. He was ordained at Ashford, Conn., in 1777; he removed thence to Grafton, Mass., in 1779, where he remained nearly three years prior to his removal to Philadelphia.

Immediately after the close of the war attention was given to fostering those interests which are vitally connected with all true growth. Hence, in the proceedings of the Association for 1782, is the following, relative to the circulation of the Bible—the Book which Baptists believe to be the only rule of faith and practice:—

A letter from Mr. Aitken, printer, in this city, was read, setting forth that he had, with great pains and much expense, just completed the first English edition of the Bible in America, together with Watt's Psalms, and requesting this Association to make the undertaking as universally known as we can.

Voted, that this Association, on the recommendation of Congress, of said impression, present their thanks to Mr. Aitken, for his faithful execution of this laborious and important undertaking, and most heartily recommend to all the churches with which we are connected, to encourage the sale therereof.

At the same session Brown University again received attention and it was

Voted, That the Association, from a representation made to them by the corporation in the college in Providence, of the low state of the funds of said college, and the urgent necessity of them, in order to support suitable instructors therein, and from an idea of the great importance of good education, have taken into consideration, as the most probable method to accomplish this end, the recommendation of a subscription throughout all the Baptist societies on this continent, as well as to all the friends of literature in every denomination, on the following conditions:—

"We, the subscribers, promise, and engage to pay, the several sums affixed to our names, to   , to be by him paid to John Brown, Esq., of Providence, Treasurer of the corporation, or his successor in said office or order; to be placed at interest, and the interest only to be applied to the above purpose."

N. B.—The several churches are desired to insert in the above blank the name of the most suitable person in the society for this service.

In the minutes of this year there is the first reference to

what is known as "The Honeywell School Fund." It is as follows:—

As we have information that a legacy has been left to this Association, in the last will and testament of John Honeywell, of Knowlton, in Sussex County, New Jersey, deceased,

Resolved, That our Treasurer, Rev. Samuel Jones, who is also in said will constituted a trustee of the same, proceed immediately, and make use of all due and necessary measures to recover said legacy for and in our behalf, and at our expense.

An outline sketch of the object and history of this legacy will here be in place. It is from the pen of Horatio Gates Jones, Esq.:—

John Honeywell, the founder of this school fund, was a resident of Knowlton township, Sussex county, N. J., and died there about the year 1780. Mr. Honeywell was once a Baptist, but, through some cause not now remembered, he was excluded from the church. His will is dated May 11th, 1779, and is recorded in New Jersey.

After providing for the support of his wife, Rebecca Honeywell, and giving several small legacies to his relatives, he directed the whole of his real estate to be sold, the proceeds to be invested and the annual income to be used for the establishment and support of a school or schools, to "be kept at the cross-roads leading from the Moravian Mills to Delaware river, near Peter Wolf's, in Knowlton township, or near the northeast corner of my land where I now live." He then adds, "my desire is that the master that is to receive his pay out of my estate may be a man of civil conduct and able to teach the boys and youth to read, write, cipher and so forth; and the mistress, likewise, to be of chaste behaviour; able, also, to teach the small girls to read, and the bigger to knit and sew and the like, so as to be a help to owners and children."

CHAPTER XIV.—1783-1790.

SCRUPLES CONCERNING LAYING ON OF HANDS.—KEEP THE ORDINANCES AS DELIVERED.—MONTGOMERY COUNTY FORMED.—PRESIDENT MANNING AND PHILADELPHIA BAPTISTS.—THE FIRST DOCTOR OF DIVINITY.—LORD'S SUPPER, AND SCATTERED MEMBERS.—LOYALTY TO THE COLONIES.—PENNYPACK CHURCH INCORPORATED.—NEGLECT OF THE LORD'S SUPPER.—STAGE TO NEW YORK.—NOT INCORPORATED.—THE TEMPERANCE QUESTION.—A BAPTIST HYMN BOOK.—REV. SAMUEL JONES, A DOCTOR OF DIVINITY.—SINGING AVOIDED.—AUTHORIZED TUNES.—REV. WM ROGERS APPOINTED TO A PROFESSORSHIP.—PLAIN FURNITURE.—ROXBOROUGH CHURCH ORGANIZED.—ABOLITION OF SLAVERY.—OLD MEETING-HOUSE AT ROXBOROUGH.

IN the Minutes of the Philadelphia Association for 1783, we have the first recorded departure, in this vicinity from the ancient custom of laying on of hands on baptized believers.

In answer to the query from Newton Church: Whether laying on of hands be an ordinance of the Gospel to be administered to all baptized persons, or only in particular cases, we observe, that imposition of hands on baptized persons has been the general practice of the churches in union with this Association, and is still used by most of them; but it was never considered by the Association as a bar of communion.

Resolved, That any person scrupling to submit thereto, may be admitted to the fellowship of the church without it.

In view of events which have since occurred in other localties, the following procedure of the Association in 1784, may be of interest. " In answer to a query from one of our churches: What measure ought to be taken with a sister church who holds and actually admits unbaptized persons to the Lord's supper? We observe, that such a church may and ought in the first instance, to be written to by a sister church, exhorting them to desist from such a practice, and to keep the ordinances as they were delivered to them in the word of God."

In 1784, Montgomery County was formed out of a part of Philadelphia, so that the history of the church of that name no longer legitimately belongs to this work.

The interest which President Manning, of Brown University, ever manifested in Philadelphia Baptists, and the respect they entertained for him is worthy of note. He was frequently here, and at the Philadelphia Association. During the five years, 1785-90, preceding his death, he attended every session. Three times he preached at the annual meetings of this body, twice he was elected Moderator, and once was its Clerk. In addition to these honors, the University of Pennsylvania at its annual commencement in 1785, conferred upon him the degree of Doctor of Divinity. He was the first, and for three years after, the only Baptist Minister in America who received this degree. The title is now more common, but never was it more worthily conferred than in this case.

In 1785, the church in Philadelphia numbered one hundred and eleven members. Some of these lived at considerable distances from the meeting-house, in the surrounding villages. The situation of these led this church to propound to the Association the following query: "Whether any of our ministering brethren can, consistently with New Testament order and our adopted discipline, administer the Lord's Supper, among any of our brethren and sisters, however numerous they may be in any one place, during the period of their remaining unorganized, or unconstituted as a distinct regular church by themselves?" This was answered, the next year, as follows:—

> First, that the Lord's Supper ought not to be administered to persons who are not members of any church, though baptized. Second, that this ordinance should not be administered to members of churches in a scattered situation, without the consent of one of those churches; but permission being first obtained, they may proceed.

Soon after the conclusion of the war with Great Britain, the Pennypack Church took steps towards becoming a chartered body, and, on March 9th, 1786, they approved a bill of incorporation, and were regularly incorporated March 28th, 1787. Under this act the pastor of the church was always a Trustee and the President of the Board, by virtue of his office. This relationship did not work well, and was therefore repealed April 12th, 1845. The corporate title now reads, " Trustees of the Baptist Church and Congregation in Lower Dublin township, in the county of Philadelphia."

The spirit of loyal adhesion to the interests of the colonies was unwaveringly maintained by the Baptist Churches of this vicinity. They were ever found on the side of Civil and Religous Liberty, and in defence of these inalienable rights, were ever ready to take a decided stand. Individuals might rebel against this position, but, without faltering, the churches even made the matter a subject for disciplinary action. Thus in the church at Lower Dublin, on the 15th of March, 1787, John Holmes reported that Joseph Inglish said he had not freedom to commune with a church that held with even defensive war, and asked the question whether he ought to be excluded? It was agreed to refer the matter to the Association, which was done at the next session in the following general yet practical query: " Whether a person declining communion with the church, be it for what cause it may, ought to be excluded, while his moral and religous character in other respects is unexceptionable!" This was answered in the affirmative. The annual meeting of the Association to which this last query was presented was held in New York, and in view of modern facilities for travel between this and that city, the following resolution on the Minutes of the Church in Philadelphia, relative to that meeting, is not without interest.

"Agreed that William Rogers be our Messenger to the Association, and that he set off in the *land stage* on Monday morning next."

This church, though existing as a branch and an independent body for ninety years, and having received several legacies, yet remained unincorporated. May 12th, 1788, it was determined to consider at the next business meeting, "the good or bad effects of being incorporated," but, on July 7th, it was decided not to get an act of incorporation. The Philadelphia Baptist Association was among the first religous bodies in America which took a decided stand on the temperance question. The following action was taken in 1788:—

> The Association, taking into consideration the ruinous effects of the great abuse of distilled liquors throughout this country, take this opportunity of expressing our hearty concurrence with our brethren of several other religious denominations, in discountenancing in future, and earnestly entreat our brethren and friends to use all their influence to that end, both in their own families and neighborhood, except when used as a medicine.

Shortly after the passage of the above, the church on Second Street "concurred with the Association in discouraging all abuse of distilled and other liquors, and every kind of excess in eating and drinking, and do desire the brethren to consider the importance and benefit of moderation in the use of all creature enjoyments, remembering the advice of the Apostle to Timothy, and to the churches on this subject." At the same session of the Association a movement was inaugurated towards the preparation of a Baptist Hymn Book. The Minutes state:—

> Our brethren Samuel Jones, David Jones, and Burgiss Allison, are appointed a committee to prepare a collection of Psalms and Hymns for the use of the Associated churches, and the churches of this and of our sister Associations are requested to conclude how many of said collection they will take, sending information to Brother Ustick, with all convenient despatch.

This book was published and went through several editions. It contained nearly four hundred hymns, and was in general use among the churches. We may here remark, relative to Samuel Jones, chairman of the above committee, and pastor of the church at Pennypack, that, at the annual commencement of the University of Pennsylvania, held the same year, 1788, the degree of Doctor of Divinity was conferred upon him.

Owing to the fearful persecutions to which Baptists had been exposed in the old world, they had become accustomed to meet as quietly as possible, so their meeting place should not be detected. Hence they came to avoid singing altogether as a part of their worship. In coming to this country, therefore, many continued to adhere to this avoidance of singing. With the progress of years a change was gradually introduced, and in the multiplicity of tunes in the latter part of the nineteenth century, it is interesting to know what "Psalm tunes" the church in Philadelphia authorized "to be sung in public worship," March 2nd, 1789. There were thirty-one in all, and are as follows:—

Common Metre. Isle of Wight, Brunswick, Coleshill, Mear, Bangor, Rochester or St. Michael, St. Humphrey, St. Martin's, Ninety-eighth, Fifth, Thirty-fourth, Suffield, Virginia.

Long Metre. One hundred-thirty-sixth, Old Hundred, Wells, New-hundred, Green's-hundred, Brookfield, Wellington, Morning Hymn, Angel Hymn, Bath, Savannah.

Short Metre. Little Marlboro, New Eagle Street, St. Thomas, Worksworth or Ailsborough, Orange.

Peculiar Metre. Lennox, Amherst.

The same month that the church decided to use the above tunes, Rev. William Rogers, their former highly esteemed pastor, was appointed Professor of English and Oratory, in the College and Academy of Philadelphia. By this institution, in July, 1790, he was honored with the degree of Doctor of Divinity. He continued to fill the position to which he was elected, with marked ability for twenty-three years; during which time he frequently preached the gospel in different places, and took a prominent part in the proceedings of the denomination, as well as of the church he had served in the ministry. The furniture, as well as the meeting-house, of this church, was exceedingly plain, and a record like the following, in the minutes of October 5th, 1789, would seem very strange in its application now:—

> Brother McLeod presents the church with a settee to be placed under the pulpit, and Brother Ustick is requested to return the church's thanks to Brother McLeod for so *handsome* an accommodation.

Some of the earliest settlers and largest landholders in the township of Roxborough and county of Philadelphia were Baptists, and the first attempt to maintain religious worship in the neighborhood was by them. Their numbers so increased and the distance at which they resided from the church on Second street was so great that measures were taken, in the summer of 1789, towards constituting a separate church; accordingly, in the minutes of the parent body, for August 3d, we find the following:—

> A request from our brethren and sisters at Roxborough for a dismission, in order that they may be constituted a church, being delivered to this church the 12th of July last, and the church agreed that they be dismissed. Bro. Ustick was requested to prepare the letter.

On Sunday, August 23, 1789, in a log school house, situated on the Ridge, below Monastery avenue, thirty-two persons were constituted as "the church of Jesus Christ, on the Ridge Road, Roxborough township." Rev. Samuel Jones, D. D., of Lower Dublin, Rev. Thomas Ustick, of Philadelphia, Rev. Thomas Ainger, of Wilmington, Rev. James McLaughlin of Hilltown, were present and participated in the public services. The names of the constituent

ROXBOROUGH BAPTIST CHURCH. 145

THE OLD MEETING-HOUSE OF THE ROXBOROUGH BAPTIST CHURCH.

BUILT 1790. REBUILT 1831. ENLARGED 1845. TORN DOWN 1868.

members, all of whom had been connected with the First Church, were as follows:—

Abraham Levering, Anna Levering, John Levering, Hannah Levering, Anthony Levering, Mary Levering, Nathan Levering, Sarah Levering, Samuel Levering, Rebecca Levering, Sarah Levering, Catherine Standland, John Righter, Cornelius Holgate, Mary Holgate, Hannah Coulston, Sarah Mathias, John Howell, Elizabeth Howell, George Sinn, Margaret Sinn, Doritha Sinn, William Holgate, Mary Holgate, Wigard Jacoby, Michael Conrad, Jane Conrad, Charles Nice, Elizabeth Yerkes, Sarah Gorgas, Sarah Lobb, Mary Stout.

The month following, September 27th, the first baptism after the organization of the church occurred, when Rev. Thomas Ainger immersed five persons in the Schuylkill river. Mr. Ainger was the first person baptized by immersion in Wilmington, Del., and during the first year of the existence of the Roxborough Church he was the stated supply of its pulpit. At the ensuing session of the Philadelphia Association this church was received and has remained connected with said body ever since. At that session the following resolution, in view of more recent events, is of importance:—

Agreeably to a recommendation in the letter from the church at Baltimore, this Association declare their high approbation of the several societies formed in the United States and Europe, for the gradual abolition of the slavery of the Africans, and for guarding against their being detained or sent off as slaves, after having obtained liberty; and do hereby recommend to the churches we represent to form similar societies, to become members thereof, and exert themselves to obtain this important object.

Shortly after its constitution, the Roxborough Church prepared for a meeting-house. A suitable lot was given by Nathan Levering, on which an edifice, thirty by forty feet, costing nearly £600, was erected. It was dedicated free of debt, October 24, 1790.

CHAPTER XV.—1791-1800.

REV. CURTIS GILBERT.—CHESTNUT HILL.—REV. THOMAS AINGER.—
DEATH OF PRESIDENT MANNING.—SUNDAY SCHOOL SOCIETY.—REG-
ULATION OF YOUTH.—DESTITUTE ORPHANS.—NOTIFICATION OF
MEMBERS RECEIVED.—SUPPRESSION OF PLAYS.—RECOMMENDATION
OR DISMISSION.—JOSEPH KEEN.—HOME MISSIONS.—DEATH OF MOR-
GAN EDWARDS.—REV. WILLIAM WHITE ORDAINED.—YELLOW FEVER.
—REV. THOMAS USTICK.—A SECOND CHURCH.—ASSOCIATION CHAR-
TERED.—CHURCHES DROPPED.—CHAINS ACROSS THE STREET.—
DEATH OF GEORGE WASHINGTON.—REV. THOMAS FLEESON AT
ROXBOROUGH.—A FORWARD MOVEMENT.—A FEEBLE FOLK.—MIS-
SIONARY EFFORTS.

ON Monday, the 9th day of January, 1791, Curtis Gilbert was ordained to the work of the Gospel Ministry, and entered at once upon the pastoral care of the church at Roxborough. The sermon was delivered by Rev. Thomas Ustick, and Rev. Samuel Jones, D. D., propounded the usual questions and gave the charge. He was a young man of much promise, but his life was short, for he died April 22nd, 1792. He was buried in the rear of where the old Meeting House stood. The marble headstone which marks his grave contains the following :—

In memory of
REV. CURTIS GILBERT.
The first ordained Minister in this
Church, who departed this life,
April 22nd, A. D., 1792,
In yonder house I spent my breath,
And now lie sleeping here in death,
These lips shall wake and then declare
Amen to truths, delivered there.

The nearest Baptist Church to Chestnut Hill, Philadelphia, was the one at Roxborough, therefore the few Baptists residing in that vicinity attended said church, and occasionally enjoyed visits from the minister who preached there. The first known record of a sermon at Chestnut Hill, by a Baptist Minister is found in the Minutes of the Roxborough Church. At the business meeting held on Saturday, April 23rd, 1791, Rev. Thomas Ainger was present, and "it was requested that he would preach at Chestnut Hill to-morrow." He complied with this request. This good man was for many years pastor of the First Baptist Church, Wilmington, Del., and at the side of its ancient meeting-house his remains repose, he having died in that city of yellow fever. The inscription on the marble slab which covers his grave reads as follows:—

> THE REV. THOMAS AINGER,
> who departed this life, September 20th, 1797.
> In the 43rd year of his age.
> Come all ye good and pious, hither come,
> And drop the tear of sorrow on his tomb,
> Deplore your loss, Ah! no, those tears refrain,
> For know your loss is his immortal gain.

The Baptist denomination and the cause of liberal education in this country met with a great loss in 1791, in the sudden death of Rev. James Manning, D. D., of Providence, R. I. This ocurred on Friday, July 29th. He was then in the fifty-third year of his age, having been President of Rhode Island College for twenty-seven years. The news of his death cast a heavy gloom over the Baptists in Philadelphia, where he was loved and honored as a great and good man. How he was revered here is attested from the fact that the largest space allotted in the Minutes of our Association for the first hundred years, in referring to a deceased minister, is given to Dr. Manning. After recording, with gratitude, "the goodness and grace of God the year past," the introduction to the circular letter for 1791 states:—

> But our joys abate while we reflect on the heavy tidings so generally mentioned in your letters, of the death of our highly esteemed and dearly beloved Brother, Dr. Manning, who, engaged in the dear-

est interests of religion, of science, and the prosperity of his country, fell from the zenith [of his glory and usefulness. In the general loss we sustain an important part. No longer shall we enjoy his able counsels, his divine and persuasive eloquence, nor his personal friendship. But while we trust he fell to rise to higher, to celestial glories and joys unspeakable, resignation becomes us. May the Lord sanctify to the churches and ministers of Christ, the awful stroke; enable us to feel, and faithfully discharge, the duties devolving on us, and imitate his example.

In 1791, Christians in Philadelphia had their attention specially turned to the Sunday-school work, and in that year the "First Day or Sunday-school Society" was formed in this city. It was composed of different religious denominations. That the Baptist church took a deep interest in this movement is evidenced not only from the names associated with it, but also because of the following incident, found in their minutes under date of January 4, 1791.

Bro. Shaw presented a number of pamphlets entitled, "An Exhortation to the Religious Education of Children," the printing of which amounted to one pound ten shillings; the church resolved that the Clerk draw an order on the Treasurer for the sum, to be paid out of the afternoon's collection.

From indications in the minutes, this church took the greatest interest in the moral and religious welfare of the young, so that we are of the opinion that the church was practically engaged in Sunday-school work much earlier than 1815, the date given as the time of the organization of the Bible school.

As early as November, 1792, the church on Second Street appointed a committee for the "regulation of the youth connected with the congregation." From this sprang in the latter part of 1795, a society in said church, "with the laudable view of educating and assisting the destitute orphans that should become members of this society, either by their own act, or that of their parents, guardians, friends, as well as for the establishing a Register of the Births and Deaths therein." This society continued till

1812, when its limits were enlarged, as we shall see hereafter. In the inauguration of other movements at this time, which have since become a part of our denomination's life and practice, this church filled a conspicuous place. The origin of a custom now universally recognized among Baptist Churches may be traced back to a query presented by this church to the Association in 1794, which is as follows: " Would it not be advisable for the churches in this connection to make it their invariable practice to transmit a return of the reception of persons by letter, to the churches by whom they were dismissed?" This question was determined in the affirmative, and now as a general thing all letters of dismission from one church to another contain this phrase or one similar:—" When (he or she) shall have been received by you, *of which you will please notify us,* said (brother or sister) will be considered as dismissed from us."

While the church was so active in these directions, it is not surprising to find her not only maintaining strict discipline amongst her own members, but also endeavouring to suppress the immoralities of the theatre. December 2, 1793, it was, " on motion, resolved unanimously, that there be a committee appointed to confer with committees from other religious societies for the suppression of plays." The committee consisted of Rev. Thomas Ustick, Rev. William Rogers, D. D., Benjamin Shaw, John McLeod, George Ingels, Heath Norbury and Joseph Keen. These brethren reported the next month, "that they met with committees appointed from the following societies, viz.: the Scotch Presbyterians, the Third Presbyterian Church, and the Methodists, who joined with them in their effort."

One name given in the above committee is deserving of special mention; that of Joseph Keen. An examination of the Minutes of the First Church gives a remarkably favorable impression of him, as a man of marked Christian character, devoted to all the interests of the church, and a worthy sire of a noble family, still identified with the denomination in this city.

The practice now prevalent of making a distinction between letters of dismission and those simply of recommendation, owes its origin to a question from this same church, in 1795. This is the query:—" Whether it might not, at this time, considering the frequency of emigration, be advisable for this Associution to insert in their minutes a request to the trans-Atlantic churches that they would be particular in their letters of recommendation and dismission of members, to specify whether they intend merely to recommend or dismiss; together with the principles and practice of the church so dismissing." An affirmative decision was given to this.

How much these movements had to do with the present education and missionary societies of our denomination cannot now be estimated, but certainly no unimportant part.

We come now to record the death of Rev. Morgan Edwards, which occurred January 28, 1795. Justice has never been done to the memory of this remarkable man. If to any one is really due the projection and *establishment* of Brown University more than to any other, Morgan Edwards is that man. As a denomination we are indebted to him for his collection of materials for early Baptist history in this country, which are now invaluable. Unfortunately for him, he became addicted to the inebriating cup, necessitating the church to resort to discipline a few years before his death, but this only continued for about four years, when he sought restoration, which was cordially granted, and up to the day of his death he lived Christ, as well as professed Him. To err is human, to forgive is divine. The greatest have sometimes fallen, but wonderful grace often saves them, nevertheless. His efforts in the Philadelphia Association, from his first entrance into it, in 1761, are manifest in the improved state and value of the minutes, and in the inauguration of various important enterprises, on to 1794, when he was present for the last time, and then "the business of the second day was opened with prayer," say the minutes, "by Bro. Morgan Edwards." In the afternoon of that day the same records state, " Minutes of this Association, from the beginning thereof to the year 1793, inclusive, bound together, were presented to the Association by Bro. Morgan Edwards. The unanimous thanks of the Association were directed to be given him for his present."

Agreeably to his own desire he was buried in the aisle of the meeting-house on Second street, where many of his family, and others also had been buried. Upon the removal of the dead from this locality, he was interred in the beautiful lot belonging to the First Baptist Church, in Mount Moriah Cemetery.

Shortly after the death of Morgan Edwards, William White was ordained in Roxborough to the work of the ministry. This was April 2nd. He was baptized in Philadelphia, March 5, 1787, and was dismissed to Roxborough, April 8, 1791, by which church he was licensed September 21, 1793. After his ordination he became pastor of the church at New Britain, Pa., where he remained for nine years.

On several occasions during this decade the yellow fever raged terribly in this city, so that the churches were materially interfered with, and the Association for four years met at a distance from the place.

We are inclined to the belief that the health of Rev. Thomas Ustick, pastor in Second street, was not very robust, as, in the latter part of the last decade, Rev. Dr. Rogers and others preached for him considerably, and he was partially laid aside from active work. In 1797, also, his church tried to secure other ministers to preach on Sunday evening. The church, however, was attached to him, and there is not in the minutes during all these years the first intimation of anything but confidence and affection. While the yellow fever raged here, Mr. Ustick was indefatigable in his efforts among the suffering. Sprague, in his *Annals of the Baptist Pulpit*,* says :—

The inhabitants were flying, panic-stricken, in every direction ; one of Mr. Ustick's friends, a highly respected gentlemen in Bucks county, requested him and his family to occupy a house in the country which he had made ready for their use; but, as his eldest daughter was, about that time, attacked by the disease, and as he could not feel willing to a separation of the family under such circumstances, he concluded to remain at his post and keep them with him, trusting to God's preserving care and goodness. During that time of peril and dismay he devoted himself, without any regard to his own safety, to the sick and dying, the great and good Dr. Rush being his companion in labour and in sorrow ; and both himself and his family were mercifully spared, though several of his children were violently attacked by the disease.

In the minutes of the church at Philadelphia, for February 6, 1796, is this record:—

A letter was presented in behalf of a people who style themselves the Second Baptist Church, in Church Alley, requesting the use of our meeting-house for evening preaching.

An answer to this was postponed till the next meeting, when the request was not complied with. There is a reference to this church again on the 8th of July. The origin and subsequent history of this party is a mystery. It certainly is not the church formerly called Northern Liberty, constituted October 29, 1769. That ceased to exist during the war, as we learn from the following minute of the Pennypack Church, under date of April 5, 1783 :—

Received Elizabeth English, she being a member of the *quondam* Second Church of Philadelphia.

---
*Page 167.

The Philadelphia Baptist Association was chartered January 24, 1797. A committee to atttend to this business was appointed in 1791. The trustees under this charter were to be the senior deacon and ministers of each church in the Association. The first meeting of this body was held in the morning of October 5, 1797. Rev. Samuel Jones, D. D., was elected President, George Ingeles, Treasurer, and Rev. William Rogers, D. D., Secretary.

In 1797 a resolution was adopted in the Association, which inaugurated a custom that still prevails. It was as follows:—

Resolved, That those churches which omit sending a messenger, or letter, to this Association for three years successively, shall be dropped from our Minutes, and considered as excluded.

In 1798, a law was passed authorizing churches in this city to place chains across the street in front of their respective places of worship, so as not to be interrupted during the service of the Lord's day, by the noise of passing vehicles. The Baptist Church with others put this law into practice, as the following Minute of May 7th, 1798, indicates:—

On motion, Resolved; that our brethren Ingels, Davis and Cox, be a committee, to carry the law lately passed, to put chains across the streets to prevent carriages passing in time of public worship, into execution.

The eighteenth century was not to close without the occurrence of an event that cast a gloom over the whole United States. This was the death, on December 14th, 1799, of George Washington, that noble man, of whom its has been said, "God left him childless in order that a nation might call him father." The mark of respect shown by the First Baptist Church to his memory, by the draping of their meeting-house in deep mourning, tells of the hold he had on the hearts of his countrymen. At the beginning of the year, January 19th, which marked the death of this great man, the Rev. Howard Malcom, D. D., since so celebrated in the missionary, educational and historical work of American Baptists, was born in this city. Rev. Thomas Fleeson, on April 26th, 1800, became a member of the Roxborough Church, and the stated supply of its pulpit for nearly a quarter of a century. He was originally connected with the church in Philadelphia, having been baptized by Rev. William Rogers, D.D., in 1774. He was licensed to preach January 9th, 1775.

About the time of his settlement in Roxborough, he lost his sight, and was thereafter known as "the blind preacher."

This city was now beginning to grow more rapidly, and the idea of extension began to take possession of the Baptists. A movement was inaugurated May 5th, 1800, towards securing a lot in what was then called the Northern Liberties, suitable for a graveyard, and to erect a meeting-house upon. The Baptist denomination, however, was still a feeble folk, numerically, as in the entire city and county they numbered only three churches with an aggregate membership of two-hundred and seventy-one.

It will be germain here to note other movements of the church in consonance with the aggressive spirit already indicated. We quote from the Association minutes for 1800:—

A query having been received from the church at Philadelphia on the subject,

Resolved, That it be particularly urged on our churches that, as stewards of God, and influenced by a strong desire to spread the cause of our blessed Redeemer, they endeavour to raise, as early as possible, and to maintain a fund for the assistance of such ministers as may be called to destitute churches, or otherwise publish the gospel in their connection, and as there are flattering prospects at the church at Manahawkin, which has been recently visited with much succcess, they earnestly entreat that some collections be immediately forwarded to Bro. Rogers for the desirable purpose of affording them ministerial aid.

Whereas, The church of Philadelphia have presented a query on the propriety of forming a plan for establishing a missionary society, this Association, taking the matter into consideration, think it would be most advisable to invite the general committtee of Virginia and different Associations on the continent, to unite with us in laying a plan for forming a missionary society and establishing a fund for its support, and for employing missionaries among the natives of our continent.

CHAPTER XVI.—1801-1806.

NEW ERA OF GROWTH.—MEASURES TOWARDS AN AFRICAN CHURCH.—
LETTER FROM WILLIAM CAREY.—A MISSIONARY SOCIETY.—BAP-
TISMS ON A WEEK-DAY.—SHADE TREES AT THE BAPTISTERION.—
JOSEPH S. WALTER.—HOLY SPIRIT POURED OUT.—SECOND BAPTIST
CHURCH CONSTITUTED.—MODERATOR SHOULD BE A MEMBER.—
A MASONIC LODGE ROOM OCCUPIED FOR RELIGIOUS WORSHIP.—
THE SECOND BAPTIST MEETING-HOUSE DEDICATED.—DEATH OF
THOMAS USTICK.—BLOCKLEY BAPTIST CHURCH CONSTITUTED.—
BUILD A MEETING-HOUSE.—SINGING LED BY PRECENTORS.—CHRIS-
TIANS IN THE CHOIRS.—REV. WILLIAM WHITE, PASTOR OF THE SEC-
OND CHURCH.—LICENTIATES' NAMES.—REV. WILLIAM STAUGHTON
IN PHILADELPHIA.—CROWDED CONGREGATION.—NEW MEETING
HOUSE AT LOWER DUBLIN.—FIRST BAPTIST MEETING-HOUSE EN-
LARGED.—FOUR SERMONS ON SUNDAY.—HORATIO GATES JONES,
D.D.—CHURCHES LIGHTED BY CANDLES.—HEATED BY WOOD STOVES.
—BLANK FORMS OF LETTERS OF DISMISSION.—FIRST COLLECTION
FOR FOREIGN MISSIONS.—NUMBER OF MEMBERS NECESSARY TO
FORM A CHURCH.—VALID BAPTISM.—CHRISTIAN MISSIONS.—REV.
JOHN RUTTER EXCLUDED.—INVALID MARRIAGES.

WITH the commencement of the nineteenth century, began a new era of growth and progress in our denominational history. Measures were inaugurated looking to the establishment of an African Baptist Church in this city. April 9, 1801, the First Church appointed a committee to consider the subject, several persons of color being members with them. The committee held several meetings, but could accomplish nothing definite. They were, therefore, discharged. In accord with the growing interest in Foreign Missions, at the session of the Association in 1801, Rev. William Rogers, D.D., read a letter from William Carey, of Serampore, relative to the work of grace in India, and from Dr. Hawes, of England, respecting promising appearances among the Hottentots, and the Minutes state: " This Association exult in every prospect of the success of the gospel, and wish the Missionaries

God speed." Steps were also in progress looking to the establishment of a Missionary Society, to send the Gospel to the destitute parts of our own country.

In the early times the ordinance of Christian Baptism seems to have been administered on a week day, and as we have seen, at the end of Spruce Street, in the Schuylkill river. Here the First Church, in 1803, had a platform erected at the water's side, so that the administrator could preach to the assembled multitudes on baptismal occasions. On this lot, in the Spring of 1802, were planted thirty-six poplar and weeping willow trees, by the celebrated Philadelphia firm of D. & C. Landreth, who engaged that, if any of the trees should die, they would replace them. At the church meeting, when the report about the trees was made April 5th, 1802, Joseph S. Walter, a name since familiar among the Baptists of this city, narrated his christian experience, and with others, was baptized the next day, at four o'clock in the afternoon.

During the year 1802, a very copious outpouring of the Holy Spirit was enjoyed in this vicinity, and numbers who had been baptized in other communities were taking up their homes in the northern and southern parts of this city, and thus the way was, under the guidance of Divine Providence, prepared for the organization of new churches.

At the advice of the First Church, February 7th, 1803, twenty members, who resided in the Northern Liberties asked for letters of dismission, that they might form a new Baptist Church in their own neighborhood. Their request was unanimously granted. The courteous application was as follows:—

Northern Liberties, Philadelphia, February 1st, 1803.

Dearly Beloved Brethren:—Having been, by the interposition of a kind providence, permitted to assemble together in society for the worship of God, from time to time, in the Northern Liberties, for these two years past, and some of us for six years upwards, our num-

SECOND BAPTIST CHURCH CONSTITUTED.

bers being small when we first met, during which time in numerous instances, the Lord, according to his promise has met with, and blessed us, and others who have occasionally been with us. In the course of the past year we have been generally privileged with the labors of one and another of our ministering brethren and many of the inhabitants in this neighborhood have been and now are disposed to hear the Gospel, we trust the Lord inclining their hearts so to do, insomuch that the place where we meet is too strait for [us. We have commended our cause to God for direction, and our minds are strongly impressed that it would be for the extension of the cause of Christ to request from you, and we do hereby request our dismission in order to be constituted into a separate body, and to endeavour through the blessing of God to raise a house for his worship in this place. Our design in this, brethren, is not to separate from your fellowship and communion, but wish still to enjoy that union which has hitherto so happily subsisted between us and to continue in the same faith and discipline that hitherto has been our guide. And, although we feel the greatest reluctance in leaving the place where we have been so often refreshed, yet the glory of God and the good of precious souls constrain us thus to lay our request before you.

Signed, Isaac Johnson, Margaret Beaks, Jacob Burkellow, Lydia West, Thomas Timings, John Ellis, Kate Burkellow, William McGee, Cornelius Trimnel, Ann Hartley, Philip Halzell, Sarah Springer, Ann King, Hannah Thomas, Elizabeth Collard, Jacob Bayer, Mary Timings, Mary Trimnel, James Wiley Jr., Isaac Car.

Under date of February 20th, the church responded through its pastor and deacons as follows :—

The Baptist Church of Christ in the city of Philadelphia, maintaining the doctrines of grace contained in the Confession of Faith adopted by the Philadelphia Baptist Association, met at Philadelphia, September 25th, 1742, together with Treatise of Church Discipline thereunto annexed.

To our ministering brethren and all who may be particularly concerned in accomplishing the wishes of our brethren, in forming and constituting a church of the aforesaid principles in the Northern Liberties of Philadelphia.

Christian Salutation.

Beloved, Whereas our brethren and sisters, [here follows their names as above given] have applied to us to be dismissed in order that they may unite together and enter into covenant in a Gospel Church State, and since it appears that their social meetings, and occasional administrations of the Gospel afford considerable prospects that they will be prospered and increased, and that the institution will promote the declarative glory of God, the increase of the Redeemer's kingdom, and their personal edification; We do hereby give our full consent and cordial approbation to the execution of said design, that they may be constituted into a separate and independent Baptist Church, holding the aforesaid principles and practices.

Wherefore, when said constitution is formed, and the aforesaid members have covenanted, they will be considered as fully dismissed from our particular care and acknowledged in said capacity. We have only to add that the aforesaid brethren and sisters are all in full communion and good standing, and that they have our fervent prayers that 'the good will of him that dwelt in the bush may be with them; that Jesus may see the travail of his soul gathered in amongst them, that God may enlarge them as Japhet, and dwell with them as in the tents of Shem. THOMAS USTICK, *Pastor*.

Thomas Shields, George Ingels, } *Deacons.*
Joseph Keen, John McLeod,

This church was constituted March 5th, 1803, with twenty members, and was received into the Philadelphia Association at its ensuing session in October, with fifty members, twenty-five of whom had been baptized since its constitution. At the same session of the Association the First Church presented the following query:—

Is it in order to have a Moderator appointed in our Association who is not a member of one of the churches belonging to it, and a delegate at the same time to the Association from the church so belonging?

Answer: This Association is not of opinion that it is strictly speaking out of order to have a Moderator appointed, who is not a member of the churches which compose this body; yet in addition to other considerations, his being unacquainted with the course of our business, and his inability, by reason of his absence, to discharge some duties which among us devolve on the Moderator in the interval of our meetings, render such a choice improper.

The Second Baptist Church met at first for worship in a Masonic lodge-room in York court. During the few months they remained, their number increased rapidly under the ministrations of John Ellis, a licentiate, aided by other supplies. Towards the latter part of the same year, in which they were constituted a separate church, the congregation had erected for their use a neat brick building, 66 by 47 feet on Budd Street, now called New Market. A lot was also marked off and fenced in for a burial ground in the rear of the meeting-house. This place of worship was dedicated December 15th, 1803. The services continued through the entire day and were conducted by Rev. Drs. Rogers and Staughton, and by Rev. Thomas B. Montayne.

At the beginning of this century the health of Rev. Thomas Ustick began to decline. Owing to the prevalence of an epidemic fever in the city, in 1802, he removed his family to Burlington, N. J. In the Baptist church of that town he preached his last sermon, with the conviction that he should never preach again. His text was, "The grace of our Lord Jesus Christ be with you. Amen." The night before his death he said to his son, "the Lord is my shield and buckler," and on the following day, April 18, 1803, he fell asleep in Jesus. Rev. William Rogers, D. D., preached his funeral sermon from the words, "Our friend Lazarus sleepeth." On account of the illness of the pastor, Dr. Rogers was requested, April 4th, to administer baptism, and, after his death, to preach for the church until January 1, 1804, for which service he was to receive "eight dollars a day." "Out of respect for their deceased brother and late pastor," the church draped its pulpit and communion table in mourning. His death was a great loss to the denomination, for he was a man of sterling piety, scrupulous fidelity, respectable talents and very companionable. He was in the fiftieth year of his age when he died, and the thirty-first of his connection with the Lord's people.

The next Baptist church constituted in Philadelphia was that at Blockley, on Sunday, June 3, 1804. The exercises were held in a school-house at the northwest corner of Fifty-second and Walnut streets. Rev. Samuel Jones, D. D., Rev. William Rogers, D. D., and Rev. William White participated in the public services of recognition. The names of the seventeen constituent members were Rev.

John Rutter, Heath Norbury, Amos Pennegar, Cornelius Bagley, William Sheldrake, John Davis, Sarah Rutter, Mary Pennegar, Elizabeth Pennegar, Susannah Norbury, Mary Oliphant, Fanny Sheldrake, Hannah Pennegar, Jerusha Davis, Sarah Bagley, Margaret Tyson, Hannah Harper. Rev. John Rutter assumed the pastoral charge of the church, which continued to worship in the aforenamed school-house until the meeting-house was erected. August 25, 1804, Mr. John Suplee gave to the church an acre of ground on which to erect a house of worship and for a grave-yard. A small one-story building was at once erected on this spot.

October 3rd this church was received into the Philadelphia Baptist Association, with sixteen members. The minutes of that body for 1804 state :—

> The church constituted the past year at Blockley, in Philadelphia County, applied for admission into this Association, which was freely granted, after they had given full satisfaction as to their faith and practice.

The singing of the congregation was usually led, at this time, by a precentor, whose seat was in front of and under the pulpit. Thus, under date of August 6, 1804, the First Baptist Church

> *Resolved*, That the committee appointed on singing be authorized to fix upon some suitable person, who is a member of this church, to lead in public singing, in case of the absence or indisposition of Bro. Bradley, and that he take his place under the pulpit.

The churches then were very careful to have not only Christians to lead in the service of song, but also members of their own particular church.

In the year 1804 Rev. William White became the first pastor of the Second Baptist Church, and for thirteen years filled that position with marked ability and success. During the period of his labors the following brethren were licensed to preach the gospel by the church : Samuel Harris, John Hewson, Richard Proudfit, Isaiah Stratton, George

LOWER DUBLIN BAPTIST CHURCH. 163

THE LOWER DUBLIN BAPTIST CHURCH.

Patterson, William E. Ashton and James Clark; and more than five hundred persons, upon a profession of faith in Christ, were baptized into the fellowship of the church.

Rev. William Staughton, of Burlington, N. J., on February 4, 1805, signified his acceptance of the request of the church on Second street to preach for them, and, on the 8th of the following April, with his wife, he was received into their fellowship by letters of dismission from the church at Burlington. He was to supply the pulpit for one year. The reason for this limit is thus given in the letter of invitation: "Upon due investigation, the church is, at present, under a few embarassments respecting their finances. Prudence, therefore, has directed them to the procuring of a supply for one year, at which time it is expected they will be both able to call a pastor and make him comfortable." The Baptists, at this time, were few, and the house of worship on Second street was a one-story building, only forty-two feet by sixty. The congregation was about the smallest in the city, and the membership of the church only 177. From the first settlement of Dr. Staughton a new era dawned. The congregation increased, and the building was soon crowded in every part with interested hearers.

In the year 1805 the church at Lower Dublin erected a new meeting-house. The principal helper in this movement was their pastor, Rev. Samuel Jones, D. D., a man who, in his day, was a noble representative of our denomination, active in all that pertained to culture and aggressive work. For some six years previous to the building of this new house there had been no special work of grace, but, commencing with 1804, there was a large and continuous ingathering of souls, which cheered alike the heart of the venerable pastor and each member of his beloved flock.

At the end of the year 1805 Mr. Staughton was called

to the permanent pastorate. Under his efficient ministry the meeting-house became too small, and early in 1808 measures were taken towards its enlargement to the size as illustrated on the eighty-seventh page of this work. During the progress of the improvements the church used the meeting-house of the Second Church in which to administer the Lord's Supper. This addition to the edifice was pushed forward with great despatch, so that the Philadelphia Baptist Association could occupy it at their annual meeting in October of that year. Dr. Staughton was an indefatigable worker. Besides the daily instruction of youth, he preached, for some time, four sermons every Lord's Day. At six o'clock on Sunday morning he preached to large congregations in the southern part of the city, near the Swede's Church, under a large beach tree, and by these missionary efforts prepared the way for the establishment of the Third Baptist Church. To his zeal and spirit is due, in a large measure, the inauguration of many educational and missionary enterprises which have grown to bless the world.

Philadelphia has ever been and still is the residence of Baptist ministers who were not pastors in the city. One of these was Horatio Gates Jones, D. D. He removed to Roxborough in the year 1805 and resided there until his death, which occurred December 12, 1853. As a result of his self-sacrificing and persistent labors the Lower Merion Baptist Church was founded September 11, 1808, and he remained its esteemed and successful pastor up to the time of his decease. He was the first chancellor of the University of Lewisburg, a constituent member of the Triennial Convention, hereafter to be spoken of, for twenty-five years the President of the Board of Trustees of the Philadelphia Baptist Association, and in other spheres served most honorably the varied interests of the denomination he loved so well. As one of the early Baptists of this city his memory will long be fragrant, and his influence potential.

The method of lighting the churches for evening service was by candles. The purchasing of the "dips" by the pound became somewhat expensive, so the First Church, under date of January 6, 1806, "*Resolved*, That the deacons be requested to procure candles by the box for the use of the meeting-house." The method of heating the building was entirely by large tin-plate wood stoves. The floors were uncarpeted, but were sanded twice each month.

The first record of a blank form for letters of dismission to unite with other churches is found in the minutes of the First Church, under date of October 6, 1806, when it was

Resolved, That Bro. Staughton be requested to draw up a form of a letter of dismission, with a sufficient number of blanks, for the purpose of being printed, and present the same at a future meeting.

In the Association this year is the first record of public collections in the churches for Foreign Missions :—

The Association recommends that collections be made in all the churches in which they have not been made, and repeated, if found convenient, where they have already been made, for assisting our brethren in Serampore in the translation of the Scriptures into the several languages of India, and that the moneys be transmitted by our next Association to our Bro. Rogers, to be, by him, deposited in the hands of Robert Ralston, Esq., to whom gratitude is due for his disinterested and obliging attention to the reception of moneys and their transmission to India.

At this same session of the Association a query was presented from the First Church, and as the same question has been discussed more recently, it will not be out of place here :—

What is the smallest number of members necessary for forming a gospel church? Answer: On this head different sentiments are entertained. Some have supposed two or three are sufficient, others have imagined five, some ten, and others twelve, because it would seem that the church at Ephesus was formed of twelve men, Acts xix: 7. The Association is of opinion, however, that much depends upon the probability of the persons living permanently together who may be about to be constituted. It appears also desirable that there be in a new settlement, where removals are frequent, at least seven, and of these two or three males.

Then, as since, the churches were agitated as to the validity of baptism administered by one of a different faith from our own. It is evident, however, that where a person is thoroughly converted and is immersed in the name of the Trinity upon a profession of Faith, the baptism is valid without any regard to the character of the administrator. The same year that the question was asked as to how many persons were necessary to form a Gospel Church, it was queried:—

Whether can an orthodox Baptist Church receive a person who has been baptized by a Tunker, Universalist, without baptizing him again? The person has renounced Universalist principles. Answer, Yes.

At the same session, the Circular letter was written by Rev. William Rogers, on "Christian Missions." It was thoroughly permeated with the true spirit of the Gospel, and discussed the subjects as follows:—

I. The principles on which they proceed.

II. The extent to which they have been carried.

III. The encouragement we possess for future exertions. This paper says:—

The Philadelphia Baptist Missionary Society, of which several of us are members, though of recent formation, has not been left to struggle in vain, brother T. G. Jones, who is our Missionary in the eastern parts of the State of Ohio, has already made a communication of agreeable tidings. In order to baptize believers in Jesus, he has led them into waters where this holy ordinance was never administered before, and on a late tour he constituted a new Baptist Church near the town of Lisbon. Numbers listened eagerly to the preaching of the cross, and in the work his heart appears to be much enlarged.

Rev. John Rutter continued in the pastorate of the Blockley Church until September, 1806, during which time he baptized sixteen persons and the church grew to a membership of thirty-three. On account of immoralities the church excommunicated him; after which he persisted in regarding himself a minister, just as though a membership in some church was not essential to any standing in the Christian Ministry. In 1807 the Association published the following :—

> The churches in our connection are notified that John Rutter, late pastor of Blockley Church has been excommunicated; they will therefore not countenance him as a preacher.

The following query from this church was also propounded to the Association, relative to him :—" Is it consistent for an excommunicated minister to perform the solemnities of marriage between persons ? Can such marriages be viewed by us, as a people, as strictly legal ? "

Answer, " The Association are of opinion that, with an excommunicated minister, we have no more to do, except as it may relate to the announcing of such excommunication; the law or any society he may join, must become the judge of his conduct; for ourselves we cannot countenance such marriages."

CHAPTER XVII.—1807-1810.

CITY PASTORS RESIDING IN THE COUNTRY.—FRANKFORD BAPTIST CHURCH CONSTITUTED.—MEETING-HOUSE ERECTED.—CENTENNIAL ANNIVERSARY OF PHILADELPHIA ASSOCIATION.—CHRONOLOGICAL LIST OF CHURCHES.—SECOND BAPTIST CHURCH INCORPORATED.—JOHN P. CROZER.—WAYSIDE EFFORTS.—THIRD BAPTIST CHURCH CONSTITUTED.—IMPOSITION OF HANDS.—FIFTEEN HUNDRED DOLLARS AND PARSONAGE.—CLOSE SUPERVISION AND STRICT DISCIPLINE.—PROHIBITION OF SOCIETY FUNERALS.—FIRST AFRICAN BAPTIST CHURCH CONSTITUTED.—HOUSE FOR BAPTISMAL OCCASIONS.—MISSIONARY SOCIETY EXTENDING ITS LABORS.

IT is sometimes regarded as a modern innovation for city pastors to reside, even during the summer time, out in the country. Dr. Staughton, when pastor of the First Church, in the summer season frequently lived some miles away. Thus in 1809 he resided in Germantown. In August, 1807, he writes, "We have this summer a beautiful situation, four miles from Philadelphia." The great demands made upon pastors of prominent city churches by visitors having every conceivable object in view, not only germain to the minister's work, but also entirely foreign thereto, are simply fearful, and when it is possible to secure a home for a pastor at a distance from the church, an improvement in pulpit efforts is generally the result.

On the 24th of May, 1807, twenty-four members were dismissed from the Second Church to constitute the Frankford Baptist Church of this city. Their names were, Thomas Gilbert, Mary Gilbert, Joseph Gilkey, John Rorer, William Phillips, Mary Phillips, J. P. Skelton, Maria Skelton, Isaac Reed, Elizabeth A. Reed, John Chipman, Elizabeth Chipman, John Dainty, Mary Dainty, James Clark, Mary Clark, Benjamin James, Sarah Lyons, Esther Gordon, Margaret Kildare, Hannah Cottman, Leah Cottman, Francis Sellers,

Phebe Davis. Six other persons, baptized by Rev. Thomas Montayne, were also regarded as constituent members.

Among the pioneer laborers in Frankford were Revs. John Ellis, T. B. Montayne, William Staughton, D. D., Samuel Jones, D. D., William Rogers, D. D., and William White.

The above little band, having no house of worship in which to gather, were consitituted into a church in a part of Nature's temple known as "Smith's Woods," situated on the Asylum Road. Here, also, they first celebrated the Lord's Supper, and on June 13, 1807, in a stream near by, three converts, Margaret Rees, Mary Coon and Dinah Thomas, were baptized. In July of the same year a lot of ground was purchased at the corner of Pine and Edwards streets for $166.66, and a substantial stone meeting-house erected thereon. In October following, the church united with the Philadelphia Association, which rendered material aid in supplying them with preaching for about two years. In 1808 an effort was made to obtain an Act of Incoporation, but for some unaccountable reason it was not obtained until 1824.

We come now to the centennial anniversary of the Philadelphia Association. One hundred years had passed since, in a small frame structure on Second street, it had been organized with only five churches, and the only body of the kind on the continent. It met in this city on the identical spot where it was formed, October 6th, 7th, and 8th, Its founders had all gone to their reward, but the work they had commenced had been carried gloriously forward. Instead of the one Association of a century ago, there were now ninety-two in the country, while the number of Baptist churches in the land had increased to nearly two thousand, and the aggregate membership to about one hundred and forty thousand. The century sermon was

CHRONOLOGICAL LIST OF CHURCHES. 171

preached by Rev. Samuel Jones, D. D., from the text, Isaiah ii : 3. " Enlarge the place of thy tents, and let them stretch forth the curtains of thy habitation. Spare not, lengthen thy cords and strengthen thy stakes, for thou shalt break forth on the right hand and on the left." The sermon is published in the minutes of the Association, and is a valuable document, by one of the most useful and honored fathers of our denomination. His services in the cause of Christ were laborious, timely and successful. An educated man himself, he was an educator in a noble sense, and to this day his influence is felt for good in many ways.

In 1807, the Association numbered thirty-nine churches with an aggregate of 3632 members. The following table exhibits the names of all the churches admitted to the Association during the first hundred years of its history, the county and state in which the churches are located, with the date of their admission to the Association:—

Church.	County.	State.	Date of Admission.
1 Lower Dublin,	Philadelphia,	Pennsylvania,	1707
2 Middletown,	Monmouth,	New Jersey,	1707
3 Piscataway,	Middlesex,	New Jersey,	1707
4 Cohansey,	Cumberland,	New Jersey,	1707
5 Welsh Tract,	New Castle,	Delaware,	1707
6 Great Valley,	Chester,	Pennsylvania,	1711
7 Cape May,	Cape May,	New Jersey,	1712
8 Hopewell,	Hunterdon,	New Jersey,	1715
9 Brandywine,	Delaware,	Pennsylvania,	1715
10 Montgomery,	Montgomery,	Pennsylvania,	1719
11 Tulpehocken,	Berks,	Pennsylvania,	1738
12 Kingwood,	Hunterdon,	New Jersey,	1742
13 Cranberry, now Hightstown,	Middlesex,	Pennsylvania,	1746
14 First,	Philadelphia,	Pennsylvania,	1746
15 Southampton,	Bucks,	Pennsylvania,	1746
16 Scotch Plains,	Essex,	New Jersey,	1747
17 Horseneck,	Fairfield,	Connecticut,	1747
18 Oyster Bay,	Queens,	New York,	1750
19 Morristown,	Morris,	New Jersey,	1752
20 Rocksberry,	Morris,	New Jersey,	1753

	Church.	County.	State.	Date of Admission.
21	Ketockton,	Loudon,	Virginia,	1754
22	Opekon,	Frederick,	Virginia,	1754
23	Harford,	Baltimore,	Maryland,	1754
24	New Britain,	Bucks,	Pennsylvania,	1754
25	Salem,	Salem,	New Jersey,	1755
26	Newton, now Wantage,	Sussex,	New Jersey,	1758
27	Bateman's Precincts,	Dutchess,	New York,	1758
28	Dividing Creek,	Cumberland,	New Jersey,	1761
29	Smith's Creek,	Frederick,	Virginia,	1761
30	First,	New York,	New York,	1763
31	Knowlton,	Sussex,	New Jersey,	1763
32	New Mills, now Pemberton,	Burlington,	New Jersey,	1764
33	Konoloway,	Cumberland,	Pennsylvania,	1765
34	Coram,	Long Island,	New York,	1766
35	Crosswicks, now Upper Freehold,	Monmouth,	New Jersey,	1766
36	Mount Bethel,	Somerset,	New Jersey,	1768
37	Lyons Farms,	Essex,	New Jersey,	1769
38	Goshen,	Orange,	New York,	1769
39	Philip's Patent,	Dutchess,	New York,	1770
40	Pittsgrove,	Salem,	New Jersey,	1771
41	Manahawkin,	Monmouth,	New Jersey,	1771
42	Vincent,	Chester,	Pennsylvania,	1771
43	Tuckahoe,	Gloucester,	New Jersey,	1771
44	Northern Liberty,	Philadelphia,	Pennsylvania,	1771
45	Cortland's Manor,	Dutchess,	New York,	1774
46	Second,	New York,	New York,	1774
47	Stamford,	Fairfield,	Connecticut,	1774
48	King Street,	Fairfield,	Connecticut,	1774
49	Oblong, now Millerton,	Dutchess,	New York,	1774
50	Cow Marsh,	Kent,	Delaware,	1781
51	Armenia,	Dutchess,	New York,	1781
52	London Tract,	Chester,	Pennsylvania,	1781
53	Hilltown,	Bucks,	Pennsylvania,	1885
24	Lower Smithfield,	Bucks,	Pennsylvania,	1785
55	Mispilion,	Kent,	Delaware,	1785
56	First,	Baltimore,	Maryland,	1786
57	Duck Creek,	Kent,	Delaware,	1786
58	First, Wilmington,	New Castle,	Delaware,	1786
59	Canoe Brook,	Essex,	New Jersey,	1786
60	Jacobstown,	Burlington,	New Jersey,	1786
61	Staten Island,	Burlington,	New Jersey,	1787
62	Pittston,	Luzerne,	Pennsylvania,	1787
63	Marcus Hook,	Delaware,	Pennsylvania,	1789
64	Roxborough,	Philadelphia,	Pennsylvania,	1789

SECOND BAPTIST CHURCH INCORPORATED. 173

Church.	County.	State.	Date of Admission.
65 Penn's Manor,	Bucks,	Pennsylvania,	1789
66 Sideling Hill, now Samptown,	Middlesex,	New Jersey,	1792
67 West Creek,	Cumberland,	New Jersey,	1792
68 Shamokin,	Northumberland,	Penn.,	1796
69 Amwell, now Flemington,	Hunterdon,	New Jersey,	1798
70 Burlington,	Burlington,	New Jersey,	1801
71 Mount Holly,	Burlington,	New Jersey,	1802
72 Dover,	York,	Pennsylvania,	1802
73 Second,	Philadelphia,	Pennsylvania,	1803
74 Second, Hopewell,	Hunterdon,	New Jersey,	1803
75 Blockley,	Philadelphia,	Pennsylvania,	1804
76 Squan,	Monmouth,	New Jersey,	1805
77 Evesham, now Marlton,	Burlington,	New Jersey,	1806
78 Trenton and Lamberton,	Mercer,	New Jersey,	1806
79 Frankford,	Philadelphia,	Pennsylvania,	1807

From the above table we learn that Philadelphia was the great centre for the churches in all the region round about. From Pennsylvania, New Jersey, New York, Connecticut, Delaware, Maryland and Virginia they came during the first hundred years of its existence, to be identified with it.

By an act of the Legislature of Pennsylvania, passed in 1809, the Second Baptist Church was regularly incorporated.

There have been born in Philadelphia many who in after years were honored of God in doing a great work for him. So there have been baptized into the churches of this city persons whose names have become household words and whose memories will be fragrant to the latest hour of time. Among these is the name of John P. Crozer, who with his sister Sarah, was baptized in the Schuylkill river, at half-past twelve o'clock on Saturday, April 9th, 1808, by Rev. William Staughton, D. D., and united with the First Baptist Church. Mr. Crozer was now only fifteen years of age, having been born January 13th, 1793. The circumstances of his conversion are thus given in the beautiful language of his biographer, Rev. J. Wheaton Smith, D. D.,* "On the farm adjoining his (J. P. Crozer's) father's lived an estimable family by the name of Pennock. On the death of a daughter in their household—a lovely Christian young woman, who was the intimate friend of Elizabeth, the sister of John,—Dr. Staughton came from Philadelphia to preach the funeral sermon. The neighbors and friends assembled at the house of the Pennocks, where the service was held. Under the influence of this and a few following discourses at the same place a number of persons were converted, among whom were John and his sister Sarah.

"Little did the excellent Staughton think, as he stood that day under the low ceiling of a farm-house room, looking around him upon the little company of neighbors and friends seated upon chairs and benches, that there sat among the boys a plain but thoughtful lad, not yet fifteen years old, who was to be one of the brightest jewels in the crown of his future rejoicing—one who would hew out a way to opulence and extended usefulness, becoming the benefactor of the poor, the friend of the 'feebleminded,' the patron of learning, and the steadfast supporter of religion. Often in after years the full, round tones of this princely preacher rung out upon the ears of the multitude which thronged his ministry in the old round meeting-house in Sansom Street; but never, perhaps, were they heard so far as when he spoke in the farm-house kitchen. As he arose, the hopes of future colleges and schools hung trembling on his words; Ethiopia was stretching out her hands to God in the prayer of that simple service; and the silver bells of Burman pagodas hung hushed and tremulous to the songs of praise.

"Brethren in the ministry of Jesus, let us take a lesson. Our wayside efforts may prove our best. A sermon in a

---

* Life of John P. Crozer, page 30.

country town, a friendly talk on the dusty path of travel, a word of counsel in some desolate household of the poor, may yield the crowning blessing of our earthly lives."

In the business meeting of the First Church, August 7, 1809, " the following letter was presented from a number of brethren, in Southwark, requesting to be dismissed in order to form a new church of our Lord Jesus Christ ":—

This is to certify that we, whose names are hereunto subscribed, have taken into consideration how desirable it would be for the Baptist cause to be extended in this city and established in Southwark, and, after due deliberation, do believe no plan more eligible could be concerted to bring about the erection of a Baptist meeting-house in Southwark than for a sufficient number of brethren and sisters unitedly to agree to be constituted into a regular church of Jesus Christ, under the name of the Third Baptist Church of Philadelphia.

We, therefore, after all due consideration, do solicit of the First Baptist Church of Philadelphia, of which we respectively stand members, a letter of dismission for the purpose of being constituted an independent church of Christ, under the name above mentioned.

We would not have any of our brethren harbor a thought that our request arises from any disaffection on our parts, nor from a wish to leave the church of which we are members from any other consideration than the advancement of the Redeemer's interest. Hoping this, our resolution, will meet your cordial approbation, and that when such a measure, with your concurrence and assistance, may be entered into, there may exist the utmost harmony and Christian love is the prayer of yours in a precious Redeemer.

Samuel Oakford, Hannah Bacon, Elizabeth Van Blunk, Richard Van Blunk, Annie Elberson, Mary Cane, Isaac Bacon, Elizabeth Merwine, Benjamin Thomson, Rachel Barber, Mary Robinson, Richard Johnson, Anna Clark, Sarah Barnet, James Naglee, Sarah Cox, Sarah James, John P. Peckworth, Jane Peckworth, Enoch Reynolds, John McCleod, Eliza McCleod, Lewis Baldwin, William Robinson, Jehu Milnor, John Cox.

This very kindly request was unanimously granted, and on Wednesday, August 23rd, they were constituted in the First Baptist meeting-house as the Third Baptist Church.

The early custom of imposition of hands on the newly baptized continued to be practiced in the First Church, under the ministry of Dr. Staughton. Under date of April 3, 1809, it is recorded :—

> John Kidwell having been baptized and expecting shortly to sail, was received by the imposition of hands, and then received the right hand of fellowship.

So prosperous had the church become that the month following the above record they were able to pledge to their pastor fifteen hundred dollars and the free use of the parsonage. While the church then, as since, was always disposed to do liberal things for their pastor, they had never previously been able to give so large a salary.

It is impossible to peruse the minutes of the churches all through the early days without being impressed with the strict discipline that was maintained by them. The utmost care was exercised in the reception of members; the closest supervision was maintained over all connected with the church, and any dereliction, or wandering, or infidelity was vigorously attended to. Everyone seemed to feel that there was a difference between a member of church and a non-professor.

It is an old and familiar adage that times change. At the present day we are impressed with this as we read a record like the following in the minutes of the First Church, under date of June 26, 1809 :—

> On motion it was resolved, that in future there shall not be any funeral in military order, that is, with arms or martial music. Funerals in Masonic order are also prohibited in our burial ground. Our sexton is desired to attend to the above resolution.

After much discussion and perplexity it was now felt that the time had fully come for the organization of an African Baptist church in this city; accordingly, under date of June 12, 1809, in the minutes of the First Church, " the following letter, dated May 13, 1809, was received from brethren of Color " :—

> We, whose names are here written, are desirous of obtaining our

letters of dismission from the First Baptist Church in Philadelphia for the purpose of becoming a distinct church of the Lord Jesus.

John Harris, Jane Simmonds, Sarah Johnson, Edward Simmonds, Hannah Cole, Zilpha Rhees, Samuel Johnson, Nancy Cole, Sarah Bartley, Sarah Harris, Phillis Dorcas, Jane Riddle, Betsey Jackson.

This request was complied with, and on June 19th, it was

Resolved, That this church give our brethren of color the use of this house on Thursday, the 29th inst., for the purpose of being, with members from other churches, constituted and organized into a regular church state.

It was further *Resolved*, That our brethren Staughton, Rogers, Peckworth and Ingels be a committee to assist our brethren of color in their constitution.

The church subsequently aided, very materially, this new organization.

July 9, 1810, the First Church authorized the erection of a two-story brick building, 32 by 18 feet, at a cost of $1,100, on the lot at Spruce street and the Schuylkill river, for baptismal occasions.

The Missionary Society of our city continued to extend its labors, and met with cheering results. October 5, 1810, the Secretary, Rev. Dr. Staughton, wrote as follows:

The Philadelphia Baptist Missionary Society announces with pleasure to the churches and to the public that there are seven missionaries at the present time in their service. Bro. Thomas G. Jones is engaged in the tract of country near the dividing line of the states of Ohio and Pennsylvania. Bro. Thomas Smiley on the western waters of the Susquehanna. Bro. Henry George is laboring on the waters of the Owl Creek, in the Ohio state; and Bro. William West on the margin of Lake Erie and the country adjacent. Bro. Montayne for two months in the year has been, and continues engaged in the small towns on the Delaware and in other parts of Bucks and Northampton counties, Pennsylvania. Brethren Bateman and Cooper, whose appointments originated at the present meeting, have their tours assigned them in parts of West Jersey where the gospel is never or seldom preached,—excepting that Bro. Bateman is instructed to devote a part of his time in Pennsylvania. The information received from the Missionaries is peculiarly encouraging; a holy zeal for the spread of the Redeemer's kingdom among us, we trust, is greatly reviving. It is hoped the churches generally will catch and retain the sacred flame, and that (to use the words of our Bro. Carey) we may be assisted to " expect great things and attempt great things."

L

CHAPTER XVIII.—1811-1815.

GROWTH OF THE CITY WESTWARD.—SANSOM STREET BAPTIST CHURCH ORGANIZED.—DR. STAUGHTON SETTLED AS PASTOR.—COLLECTIONS AT THE LORD'S SUPPER.—REV. JOHN P. PECKWORTH.—REV. DAVID JONES, JR., AT FRANKFORD.—REV. HENRY HOLCOMBE, D. D., PASTOR OF FIRST CHURCH, PHILADELPHIA.—MISSIONARY SPIRIT.—A PRINCETON STUDENT BAPTIZED.—A SCRIPTURAL RIGHT TO BAPTIZE.—REV. JOHN KING.—BAPTIST ORPHAN SOCIETY.—EMPORIUM OF BAPTIST INFLUENCE.—FIRST AMERICAN MISSIONARIES.—PHILADELPHIA BAPTIST SOCIETY FOR FOREIGN MISSIONS.—A CONSECRATED SPOT.—TRIENNIAL CONVENTION.—NAMES OF DELEGATES.—DEATH OF DR. SAMUEL JONES.—SUNDAY SCHOOLS ORGANIZED.—HISTORY OF THE FIRST CHURCH BIBLE SCHOOL—HISTORICAL ADDRESS BY JUDGE HANNA.

THE growth of the city westward, and owing to the size of the First Church, then numbering 473 members, steps were taken at the beginning of January, 1811, towards the organization of a new church. Nearly one hundred members were dismissed. At first this movement seemed to be approved by all parties, but unfriendly remarks were made, which inaugurated a spirit of alienation, whose bitter results have since been sorrowfully learned. No good ever comes from crimination and recrimination. A guarded tongue and a quiet peace-making conduct are always commendable in all enterprises, especially in connection with the interests of the Redeemer's kingdom. This movement resulted in the organization of the Sansom Street Baptist Church, on the 24th of January, 1811, and the following month Rev. Dr. Staughton was called as pastor. This call he accepted. The church worshipped for a time in the court-house on Chestnut Street, and afterwards in the Academy on Fourth Street. A lot, however, was soon procured on Sansom Street, above Eighth, whereon was erected a circular building, ninety feet in diameter, which, with the lot, cost the sum of $40,000.

DR. STAUGHTON SETTLED AS PASTOR. 179

"Large as this amount was," * says the Memoir of Dr. Staughton, "the probability is that it would have been obtained, had not adverse circumstances occurred, producing great commercial distress. The annual revenue arising from pew rents and collections amounted at first to between four and five thousand dollars. The seats of this immense building, during the whole period of his ministrations, were well filled; but, on the Lord's day evening, the place was crowded with solemn and admiring spectators. His popularity was unimpaired by time, and those who heard him once desired to hear him again. With this church he spent the happiest and most useful days of his life."

It is now universal among Baptist Churches to take up a collection after the administration of the Lord's supper, for the poor of the church. The first introduction of this custom in this vicinity was authorized by by the First Church, January 11th, 1811, after several months discussion, as follows; " It was resolved that a collection for the use of the poor members of this church be made monthly, immediately after the hymn is sung, at the conclusion of the administration of the Lord's Supper." At the organization of the Third Baptist Church, Rev. John P. Peckworth became the pastor and filled that position for about fifteen years, during which time the church prospered greatly under his ministry. He was highly esteemed by all the churches, and faithfully served the cause of Christ.

In September, 1811, Rev. David Jones, Jr., became the first pastor at Frankford. An interesting biographical sketch of this brother is published in Tract 132 of the American Baptist Publication Society. From it we quote the following relative to his labors at that place :—

It is now more than six months (May 16, 1812,) since I came to Frankford. I have endeavored to preach frequently since I came, for

---
* Page 84.

the Apostle saith, 2 Cor. 9: 6, "He that soweth *sparingly*, shall reap sparingly. The little church labors under grievous difficulties; nevertheless, I have found much freedom in dispensing the word of life among them. Our congregation is increasing.

The following entry is made at the close of his labors with this church, in his journal, dated December 13, 1813 :—

This evening I preached for the last time in Frankford. The meeting-house was crowded. I spoke from Proverbs 23 : 23. May the Lord grant to bless Frankford, and call many sinners to the knowledge of the truth. Amen. D. JONES.

He was born in North Wales, England, April 9, 1785. After leaving Frankford he became pastor in Newark, New Jersey, and remained there until December, 1821, when he assumed the pastoral care of the Lower Dublin Church, of this city. Here he labored till his death, which occurred April 9, 1833.

The First Church, left pastorless, at once looked out for a man who, in talent and commanding influence, would be a worthy successor of a noble line of able men. Rev. Dr. Broaddus, of Caroline county, Virginia, was earnestly sought, but, on account of various domestic claims, he declined. Rev. Dr. Henry Holcombe, of Savannah, Georgia, was then invited, and after preaching to the people with great acceptance he was unanimously chosen to the pastorate, October 17th, 1811. This call he at once accepted, and entered upon his duties the beginning of the new year. The church furnished his house and gave him a salary of $1,600 a year. It was customary then for the ministers to preach three times on the Lord's Day, but the church assured Dr. Holcombe that he should only preach twice. He was a man of excellent talents, strong will, vigorous in his opposition to what he supposed to be wrong, and very earnest in controversy. He ably served the First Church for thirteen years, and had within its fellowship a host of devoted and true friends.

The missionary spirit was now beginning to manifest itself, and in 1812 a monthly concert of prayer was begun by the Baptist churches of this city. The meetings were held in each church alternately, to pray "for the spread of the ever-blessed gospel." In addition to this, the churches themselves held "quarterly prayer-meetings for the spread of the gospel," at the residences of the members. March 15th, 1813, is the first recorded special sermon in the interests of Foreign Missions. The record is as follows :—

Resolved, That an appropriate sermon be preached and a collection made on Lord's day evening next, for the purpose of assisting the Mission at Serampore towards reimbursing the loss by the late conflagration.

On Saturday, October 17th, 1812, Thomas Stewart, of Beaufort, South Carolina, a student of Princeton, New Jersey, visited Dr. Holcombe, and, giving evidence of a change of heart was baptized the same day. Desirous of uniting with the church, and being under the necessity of returning at once to Princeton, to resume his studies the next morning, the pastor detained the church, when Mr. Stewart narrated his Christian experience, was received as a member, and the right hand of fellowship was at once given. A Baptist minister has a scriptural right to baptize any one giving an evidence of his faith in Jesus, but it requires a vote of the church to make said person a member. The ordinance of baptism seems to have been committed by our Lord to the ministry, and on this principle Dr. Holcombe proceeded.

In 1812 the First African Church settled as their pastor John King, one of their own licentiates. He was ordained and remained pastor for two years, when he was excluded from their fellowship.

In the year 1812 the society formed in the First Baptist

Church, with the laudable view of educating and assisting the destitute orphans, was enlarged so as to embrace all the city. Article I of the Constitution of "The Philadelphia Baptist Orphan Society" was as follows :—

The design of this Society is to establish a register of the births and deaths of members of the Baptist churches and congregations in the city and liberties of Philadelphia, who shall become subscribers thereto, and who shall pay, or cause to be paid, or have heretofore paid at the time of subscribing a sum not less than fifty cents for each name recorded in the Register. The interest arising from which fund shall be applied to the education and assistance of such orphan and indigent children whose names may have been recorded in the Society.

Under date of November 25th, 1812, the President, Thomas Shields, stated :—

The funds of this Society have increased to the amount of about $1,100, and had not the deaths of most of the Trustees been experienced, and other causes existed to retard the operation of the Society, a much larger sum would now have been at their disposal.

As a stimulus to future exertions, and with a view to concentrate the efforts of the different congregations of our denomination, it has been agreed that a union of all the churches and congregations in this city should take place, with a view of embracing the valuable purposes of establishing a record of all the births and deaths in our several congregations, and an academy for the education of our children generally, as well as the destitute orphans who will be educated and assisted according to the ability of the Society. The great utility of such a record in a Baptist Association must be obvious to every reflecting mind; not having any ceremony performed on our children in a state of infancy which is recorded as a public act—their births and deaths being recorded in a family Bible. And, in how many instances does it occur that this is either lost or destroyed; or how easy a matter it would be for a person against whom this record would operate to effectually prevent its being brought forward, by secreting or destroying it. Should we or our children wish to procure from public record our parentage or place of nativity for the purposes of obtaining a protection to go to a foreign country, or for substantiating titles to property, we have none to resort to to obtain the desired proof. And further, when we contemplate the many advantages, both temporal and spiritual, which, under the blessing of God, will arise from the establishment of a Baptist academy, that, from a small beginning, may rival any on our continent, we feel a pleasure the duty has devolved on us to assist in the establishment and support of so excellent an institution.

EMPORIUM OF BAPTIST INFLUENCE. 183

Rev. David Benedict, D. D., writing of this period, says that* "Philadelphia, both by the North and South, was regarded as the emporium of Baptist influence. Here the missionary spirit which had been kindled in different parts of the country burst forth into a flame, and here was organized The General Missionary Convention of the Baptist Denomination in the United States of America for Foreign Missions."

Early in 1812 the first American Missionaries sailed for their work in Asia. Revs. Adoniram Judson and Samuel Newell sailed from Salem on the 19th of February, and on the 24th, Revs. Messrs Hall and Nott, with their wives, and Rev. Luther Rice, sailed from Philadelphia, in the ship *Harmony*. These missionaries were Congregationalists, but on the voyage the views of Judson and his wife, and of Luther Rice, underwent a change on the subject of baptism, and they were baptized at Serampore, by Rev. Mr. Ward, of the English Baptist Mission. Judson remained, but Rice returned to stir up American Baptists to undertake the Foreign Mission work.

On Thursday afternoon, October 5th, 1813, the Philadelphia Association had this subject before them, resulting in the inauguration of active measures for the benefit of the heathen. It was determined to organize "The Philadelphia Baptist Society for Foreign Missions," and "brethren Holcombe, Staughton, Rogers, Samuel Jones, H. G. Jones, J. B. Montayne, J. Mathias, J. P. Peckworth, Joseph Maylin, W. Magee and G. Ingels" were appointed to devise a plan for the society, and to carry it into effect.

Thus the missionary spirit began to be aroused, and with that also a desire for crystalization. Delegates from local missionaray societies and other religious bodies con-

---

* Fifty Years Among the Baptists. Page 46.

vened on the 18th of May, 1814, in the meeting-house on Second Street, "to organize a plan for eliciting, combining, and directing the energies of the whole denomination in one sacred effort for sending the glad tidings of salvation to the heathen, and to nations destitute of pure gospel light." The site of this meeting was already a consecrated spot. Here the First Baptist Association of America had been organized. Here Hopewell Academy and Brown University, our first educational institutions in this country, had been projected. Here the oldest Baptist Association in the country had "met at sunrise" when the news of the surrender of the British arms at Yorktown, in 1782, was received. Fitting place for the assembling of the men who were to organize for our Foreign Mission work. There were twenty-six clergymen and seven laymen from eleven different states and from the District of Columbia. Their names are on the records in the following order:—

Rev. Thomas Baldwin, D. D.,	Massachusetts.
" Lucius Bolles, A. M.,	"
" John Gano, A. M.,	Rhode Island.
" John Williams,	New York.
Mr. Thomas Hewitt,	"
" Edward Probyn,	"
" Nathaniel Smith,	"
Rev. Burgiss Allison, D. D.,	New Jersey.
" Richard Proudfoot,	"
" Josiah Stratton,	"
" William Boswell,	"
" Henry Smalley, A. M.,	"
Mr. Matthew Randall,	"
" John Sisty,	"
" Stephen Ustick,	"
Rev. William Rogers, D. D.,	Pennsylvania.
" Henry Holcombe, D. D.,	"
" William Staughton, D. D.,	"
" William White, A. M.,	"
" John P. Peckworth,	"
" Horatio G. Jones,	"
" Silas Hough,	"

DEATH OF DR. SAMUEL JONES. 185

Rev. Joseph Matthias,	. . .	Pennsylvania.
" Daniel Dodge,	. . .	Delaware.
" Lewis Richards,	. . .	Maryland.
" Thomas Brooke,	. . .	"
" Luther Rice, A. M.,	. . .	District of Columbia.
" Robert B. Semple,	. .	Virginia.
" Jacob Grigg,	. . . .	"
" James A. Ronaldson,	. .	North Carolina.
" Richard Furman, D. D.,	. .	South Caroiina.
Hon. Matthias B. Talmadge,	. .	"
Rev. W. B. Johnson,	. . .	Georgia.

After much deliberation and prayer they organized the Triennial Convention. The object of it was for missionary purposes alone. Its meetings were held every three years, and from it has sprung our present American Baptist Missionary Union, which, under God, is doing a grand work in the heathen world. Two months prior to the meeting of this body, on February 7th, our denomination met with a serious loss in the death of Rev. Dr. Samuel Jones, at Lower Dublin, aged 79 years. He was a man of fine physical appearance, superior mental abilities, kind hearted, and had a deservedly high reputation as a preacher. He was an ornament to the denomination he served so faithfully, and to him we owe a debt of gratitude for the services he rendered with so much devotion and ability.

The year 1815 introduces us to the practical beginning of the Sunday-school work of the churches in this city; that of the First Church leading the way. Shortly afterwards and during the same year, a Sunday-school was started in the Sansom Street Church; meeting with favor, the next year one was organized in the Second Church, and in 1817, the one at Roxborough. The following year, three additional schools were started by the Third, Blockley and Fourth Churches. On account of the importance and results of this work a somewhat full account of the origin of the First Baptist School in this city will be of interest.

In 1815, Mrs. Ann Rhees, a member of the First Church, became acquainted with a poor family in the vicinity of her home, consisting of a mother and three children, whose husband and father had, a short time before, enlisted in the state service, leaving them without support, except the scanty pittance of his half pay and what little the poor mother could earn from washing. The children were growing up in ignorance. The excellent common school system now enjoyed was not then in vogue. Under these circumstances it occurred to Mrs. Rhees that for the sake of these children and others, it would be well to open a Sunday-school in the church, to teach them how to read, so they could read the Bible, and for their religous instruction. She suggested her plan to two sisters of the church, who favored the movement and agreed to co-operate. These three, Mrs. Rhees, and the Misses Mary Hallman, and Emily Ramage, at once sought the advice of a few brethren. The first one, regarded as a wise and prudent counsellor, told them "he did not like the idea of congregating children in a mass, and exhibiting them on the Lord's day to be gazed at as paupers." At this day such advice seems astounding. Caution and prudence, when balanced by a strong faith and an enterprising spirit are well, but when they exist alone, to follow them generally means inactivity, covetousness and spiritual barrenness. By this cold and cutting remark of the venerable brother, the ardor of the women was somewhat dampened, but not enough to lead them to abandon the project. They then called on their Pastor, Rev. Dr. Holcombe. He listened to their statement, and then pleasantly replied, "Well my sisters, you can but try it, blossoms are sweet and beautiful even if they produce no fruit." Cheered by this remark, and hopeful that the blossom of their consecrated effort would develope into a blessed fruitage, they called on Deacon Joseph Keen. He entered into full sympathy with their work and heartily said "Yes, my sisters. I'll do all I can to help you." He even promised to come and open the school with prayer. I cannot refrain from speaking further of Brother Keen, whose earnest words of Christian cheer were in reality the means of inaugurating the First Baptist Sunday-school of Philadelphia. No one can peruse the Minutes during his long connection with the church without being impressed with the variety and intensity of his Christian activities, the kindliness of his heart, the loyalty of his faith, and the high esteem in which he was held by the entire church. He was a worthy sire of a posterity still nobly identified with our churches in this city. Thus cheered, these women began the work of collecting the children, and on a pleasant Sunday in October, with an additional colaborer, Mrs. Sarah Ogden, held the first session of a Sunday-school under Baptist auspices in Philadelphia. Deacon Keen was true to his promise, and opened the school with the first public prayer connected with the Baptist Sunday-school enterprise of this city. With twenty boys and girls, and four female teachers, encouraged by the presence of Deacon Keen, and a friend who accompanied him, commenced that movement which has been so signally blessed of God, until in this city, in sixty years afterwards, we have sixty-five Baptist Sunday-schools, numbering 1,645 officers and teachers, and 17,561 scholars; not to speak of the immense amount of good done here and abroad through the school started in the old meeting-house, on Second Street. To this school Mrs. Rhees from the first took her two sons, Morgan J. and John. The former became an honored and useful minister of Christ, and the latter a physician. The children met at first in the gallery of the church, and were divided into four classes, taught by the above teachers. Deacon Keen went every Sunday for a time, to open the school with prayer, or to see that it was done. In his historical address, at the fiftieth anniversary of this school, Judge T. Brantly Hanna, of this city, to whom I am indebted for the facts concerning the origin of this school says: "The enterprise soon began to attract the attention of other members of the church. More teachers were enlisted, and the children of Mrs. Rhees, together with those of some courageous members who did not fear their offspring would be considered paupers, having entered the school, induced other parents to imitate their example. The school was soon taken under the fostering care of the "Female Benevolent Society," who, on the 15th of January, 1816, applied to the church for the use of the room, in the two-story building lately finished, adjoining the meeting-house, for the purpose of establishing there the Sunday School. The application was granted and the school removed to their new home, there to meet, with a short interval elapsing, when they occupied the second story of one of the stores on Second street until May, 1856, when the church took possession of the edifice at Broad and Arch streets. From the commencement, until about the close of 1818, the school was conducted mainly by the ladies."

In 1819, the Sunday-school of the First Baptist Church having been established beyond the peradventure of an experiment, the friends of the measure organized "The Sunday-school Society of the First Baptist Church and Congregation of Philadelphia." Rules and regulations for the government of the society were adopted. These were at once printed. The officers elected were as follows:—

Superintendent, James M. Bird; Assistant Superintendent, William Ford; Directress, Miss Susan Ingels; Assistant Directress, Miss Mary Hallman; Treasurer, Mrs. Margaret Garrett; Secretary, Miss Jane Garrett.

CHAPTER XIX.—CONCLUSION.

PROMINENT INCIDENTS AND PERSONS.—REV. JACOB GRIGGS.—REV. WILLIAM E. ASHTON.—REV. WILLIAM WILSON.—REV. J. C. MURPHY. —DEFECTION OF WILLIAM WHITE.—REV. JAMES McLAUGHLIN.— THE FOURTH BAPTIST CHURCH CONSTITUTED.—MEETING-HOUSE ERECTED.—THE LATTER-DAY LUMINARY.—FIRST THEOLOGICAL SEMINARY.—GRADUATING CLASSES.—COLUMBIAN UNIVERSITY.—A FEW HONORED NAMES.—J. H.KENNARD.—DANIEL DODGE.—WILLIAM J. BRANTLY.—RUFUS BABCOCK.—K. A. FLEISCHMAN.—GEORGE B. IDE. —JAMES M. LINNARD.—JOSEPH TAYLOR.—WILSON JEWELL.—DAVID JAYNE.—FRANKLIN LEE.—W. H. RICHARDS.—THOMAS WATTSON.—J. P. SHERBORNE.

IT is not our purpose to pursue the full and continuous history of the early Baptists of this city beyond the point reached in the previous chapters. Questions and difficulties are encountered during the next few years which can be written about by the historians a few years hence better than now. A few prominent incidents and persons deserving special mention will be noticed in this concluding part of our work.

In December, 1815, Rev. Jacob Grigg became pastor at Lower Dublin, succeeding the lamented Dr. Samuel Jones, who for fifty-one years had been the revered shepherd of that flock. Mr. Grigg was a man of remarkable mental powers, and it is said that, while on the voyage from England to this country, he committed to memory the entire Bible. He remained at Pennypack until September, 1817. The Blockley Church, after the removal of their first pastor in 1806, depended mainly upon supplies for the next ten years. The principal ones being John P. Peckworth, John Huson, Daniel James and Daniel Sweeney. In January, 1816, Charles Summers became the pastor, but he only remained till the following May. He was succeeded by the

Rev. William E. Ashton, who remained until September, 1822. Born in this city, May 18, 1793, Mr. Ashton was a man of fine culture, unceasing industry, and highly esteemed for his many excellent traits of character.

In 1816, after several ineffectual attempts to obtain a pastor, the Frankford Church succeeded in settling Rev. William Wilson. He only remained, however, until November, 1817. He was succeeded the ensuing month by Rev. John C. Murphy, who remained until January, 1820. The growth of the church through these years was slow but constant. Previous to settling at Frankford, Mr. Murphy supplied, for nearly a year, the pulpit of the church in Roxborough, during which time he was the means of establishing the Sunday-school in that place.

Owing to the defection of William White, late pastor of the Second Baptist Church, it seemed difficult to obtain a successor in whom all could happily unite. Hence, it was thought best that a new church should be formed. In August, 1817, Rev. James McLaughlin was elected pastor, and immediately afterwards seventy-six persons were dismissed for the purpose of entering a new organization. On the 10th of September, in the meeting-house of the Second Church, these were constituted as the "New Market Street Baptist Church, in the Northern Liberties of Philadelphia." This is now known as the Fourth Church, located at Fifth and Buttonwood streets. The sermon was preached by Rev. John P. Peckworth from 1 Peter ii: 5. Rev. Dr. Staughton propounded the necessary interrogatories then usual at such times, and Rev. Dr. Allison delivered the charge to the church. At the first meeting for business the Rev. Jacob Grigg was elected pastor. He resigned the charge of the church at Lower Dublin and entered at once upon the duties of his new field. Among the first acts of the church was the appointment of a committee to select a suitable site for the erection of a house of worship. They recommended the purchase of the lot at the corner of " Fifth Street, and Buttonwood Lane," but the location was not regarded as sufficiently eligible, being too far out of town. Accordingly a lot was secured on New Market street, above Willow.

Just one month after the constitution of the church, October 11th, the corner stone of their new meeting-house was laid. On this stone the name of the church and pastor were engraved. By the 27th of December the building was in readiness for public worship, and on the first day of January the edifice, 60 feet by 54, was dedicated to the worship of God. Sermons on the occasion were preached by Revs. T. B. Montayne and Dr. Staughton. After a pastorate of a year and a half, which was attended with signal prosperity, Mr. Grigg resigned and went to Virginia.

In February, 1818, we meet with the beginning of Philadelphia Baptist journalism. " The Latter-Day Luminary," a quarterly religious miscellany, was then begun. It was issued "by a committee of the Baptist Board of Foreign Missions." Rev. Luther Rice, the agent of said Board, appears to have been the mover and business manager of the enterprise, while Dr. Staughton, Corresponding Secretary of the Board, was the editor up to and including 1821. By this time it had attained a circulation of about 3,000 copies, when it was removed to Washington, where it was subsequently published until the close of 1824, when it was discontinued. It is a work of much vlaue, as it contains information relating to the current history of the denomination nowhere else to be found.

In 1818 the Board of the Triennial Convention organized in this city an institution for furnishing theological instruction to young men intending to enter the Christian ministry. Dr. Staughton was its President, and Professor Irah Chase was associated with him in the work. This was, in reality, the first theological seminary inaugurated by the denomination in this country. It was situated at the northwest corner of Eighth and Sansom streets, Philadelphia. A history of this institution, by Professor Chase, was published in the "American Baptist Memorial," April 15th, 1842. From that article the following will be of interest:—

The first theological class consisted of William E. Ashton, Peter Chase, Isaac Merrimam, Alvah Sabin, and Adam Wilson. Their course was terminated by a public examination, and other appropriate exercises, at the time of the annual meeting of the Board, April 25, 1821. Mr. Wilson had occasion to repair to a field of labor at a somewhat earlier day. The order of exercises included the following essays:—

1. On some of the causes which prevented a complete Reformation in the time of Luther;—by Mr. Ashton.
2. Translation of the forty-ninth Psalm, with critical remarks;—by Mr. Chase.
3. On the proper mode of interpreting parables;—by Mr. Merrimam.
4. Interpretation of 1 Cor. 10: 10;—by Mr. Sabin.
5. On the phrase, Son of God;—by Mr. Merrimam.
6. On the importance of applying to theology the Baconian principles of Philosophizing;—by Mr. Chase.
7. On the connection between a preacher's general character and the efficacy of his public instructions;—by Mr. Ashton.

"The impressions made on this occasion," says an account published at the time, "were, in no ordinary degree, gratifying and encouraging to the heart that prays, *thy kingdom come.* The whole became the more interesting from the consideration that the *first* class from the institution, was then seen going forth in the name of the Lord."

The second theological class consisted of Allen Brown, Spencer Clack, Harned, John C. Harrison, Henry Keeling, Samuel W. Lynd, Samuel Wait, and David M. Woodson. Their course was brought to a close with the close of the summer term, on Wednesday, the 25th of July, 1821. The forenoon was occupied in a public examination. In the afternoon, a meeting was held in the Sansom Street meeting-house, when, after prayer by the Rev. Mr. Rice, essays were read to an attentive assembly.

1. On the moral tendency of the distinguishing doctrines of the gospel;—by Mr. Harrison.

2. On the choice of texts for sermons;—by Mr. Harned.
3. On the proper treatment of the difficulties which occur in Revelation;—by Mr. Keeling.
4. On the use which a preacher should make of a knowledge of the original languages and learned criticisms;—by Mr. Wait.
5. On the character and offices of the Holy Ghost;—by Mr. Clack.
6. On the objection that Herod's slaying the children at Bethlehem, as stated in Matt. 2: 16, is not mentioned by Josephus;—by Mr. Brown.
7. On preaching Christ crucified;—by Mr. Lynd.

The Rev. Dr. Staughton then delivered a charge to the class, and closed the services by prayer and a benediction.

So much success attended this theological school that the expediency of attempting the organization of a college at some central point, from which a beneficial influence might go forth to every part of the land, was duly considered. The project met with favor, and Washington, D. C., was determined upon as the most eligible place. In 1819 property was purchased there for Columbian College. In February, 1821, a charter was procured from Congress, and the Institution at Philadelphia was removed to Washington, in the autumn of that year, to form the Theological Department of the College, with Professor Chase and eight students to begin with. The College, itself, with Dr. Staughton as its President, was opened in 1822. Thus this College, now called Columbian University, had its beginning in Philadelphia, the goodly city where the first Association of Baptist Chnrches was formed; where the first Latin school among the Baptists of America was inaugurated; where Brown University, our oldest institution of learning, was projected; where the Missionary Union for religious work among the heathen was organized, and where the first Theological seminary in America was established.

It would be very agreeable to take up the names of many noble men of our city who subsequently carried forward most nobly the work previously begun; ministers

M

FIRST BAPTIST CHURCH, BROAD AND ARCH STREETS.

and laymen who, having served well in the Lord's vineyard, now rest from their labors. This was not comprehended in the object of our work. A few honored names of great prominence deserve notice.

Rev. Joseph H. Kennard, D. D., was a man whose memory is still fragrant in all this region. He was the founder of the Baptist Ministerial Conference of this city, and was identified with other denominational agencies in such a way as to infuse into them his noble spirit and missionary zeal. On October 1, 1823, he enterered upon the pastorate of the Blockley Church, and from that time until his death triumphant, which occurred June 24, 1866, he was present at every session of the Philadelphia Association, and at every session took some prominent part. The Tenth Baptist Church, which he was the means of organizing, and which he served as pastor for nearly thirty years, is, indeed, a monument to his Christian integrity and hearty devotion to the kingdom of Jesus.

Then, too, there was Daniel Dodge, of the Second Church, that tower of strength in our Baptist Zion; Dr. William J. Brantley, the elder, of the First Church, that courteous, devoted and able minister of the New Testament; Rufus Babcock, D. D., of the Spruce Street Baptist Church, whose christly, evangelical spirit has been helpful to so many in their heavenward pathway; Konrad A. Fleischman, of the First German Church, a perfect John the Baptist in rugged energy and earnest interest for the salvation of his countrymen; George B. Ide, D. D., that polished preacher and faithful pastor, under whose leadership the First Church removed from Second street to Broad and Arch; and a large number whose names are embalmed in the hearts of a grateful people. Among the laymen the names of James M. Linnard, Dr. Wilson Jewel, Joseph Taylor, David Jayne, Franklin Lee, W. H. Richards, T. P. Sherborne, and a host of other Christian men might be mentioned. Their names are still revered in many households throughout this city. May their examples inspire the present membership of our churches to even greater undertakings in consecration to the cause of our Lord Jesus Christ.

INDEX.

A

Adams, John, against the Baptists, 114-116.
African Church, proposed, 157; First constituted, 176.
Ainger, Thomas, 146; preaches at Chestnut Hill, 148; death of, 148.
Allison, Burgis, at Pennypack, 107; patriotism of, 120.
Andrews, Jedediah, the Preseyterian pastor, 32.
Ashton, William E., 164, 190.
Association, Philadelphia, organized, 44; meets twice a year, 107; meets in New York, 97; no meeting of, 121.

B

Babcock, Rufus, 195.
Backus, Isaac, in Philadelphia, 108, 109.
Baptism, first record of, 23; a prerogative of the ministry, 90; precedes the Lord's Supper, 139-on a week-day, 158; validity of, 167.
Baptist history, 30, 31.
Baptist hymn book, 142.
Baptisterion, 133.
Baptists, origin of, 18; and the Romanists, 63; and religious liberty, 64; and the American Revolution, 118.
Barbadoes lot, 31; storehouse, 32.
Benedict, David, quotations from, 19, 25, 183.
Bible, circulation of, 137.
Blockley church, constituted, 161; constituent members, 162; meeting-house, erected, 162; pastors of, 189.

Brandywine Church organized, 54.
Brantley, William T., 23, 195.
Brewhouse, worship in, 34.
Brown University, 85, 96; aided, 137.
Bucks County, line of fixed, 19.
Burrows, John, 48, 49.

C

Calendar, change of, 24.
Carpenter's Hall, 108.
Catechetical instruction, 66.
Catechism published, 29.
Century Sermon, 44; Minutes, 45; first concluded, 129.
Chains across the streets, 154.
Challis, J. M., 24.
Chase, Irah, 192.
Church Discipline, treatise on, 68.
Church, number needed to constitute a, 166.
Churches, names of dropped, 154; lighted by candles, 166; heated by wood stoves, 166; chronological list of, 171.
Chestnut Hil, first sermon at, 148.
Christ Church, 38.
Circular Letter, the first, 60.
City pastors, residing in the country, 169.
Clayton, Thomas, proposition of, 35.
Cohansey Church, 25.
Cold Spring, 19; preaching at, 28; Church at 18.
Church disbanded, 42.
Collections to aid Missions, 155.
Colonies, on the side of, 120.
Columbian University, 192.
Commandment, the Fourth in force, 57.
Committee on Grievances, 110.
Communion Service of First Church, 79.

INDEX.

Conference meetings, 25.
Confession of faith, published, 29; of Philadelphia Association, 67.
Continental Congress, 108; address to, 110-114.
Convention, Triennial 164.
Correspondence with Associations, 94.
Crozer, John P., 173.

D

Davis, David, arrives, 47.
Davis, John, ordained, 75; pioneer in Maryland, 75.
Davis, William, a troubler, 28; disabled, 28.
Deacons, ordinations of, 91.
Decision, unanimity in, 58.
Discipline, treatise on, 68; strict, 176.
Division, a painful, 48.
Doctor of Divinity, the first Baptist, 140.
Doctrinal Sermon, 78.
Dodge, Daniel, 194.
Drunkenness, discipline for, 83.
Dungan, Thomas, at Cold Spring, 18; death of, 25; an ancient disciple, 26; posterity of, 26.

E

Eaglesfield, George, 58.
Eatons, arrival of, 21.
Eaton, George, 71; called to preach, 75, 88; preaches at Roxborough, 88; death of, 88.
Eaton, Isaac, 71, 73; last sermon of, 105.
Eaton, Joseph, ordained, 59; heterodox, 69; death of, 73.
Edwards, Morgan, quotations from, 18, 22, 24, 26, 27, 31, 39, 41, 45, 65; the historian, 30; invited from England, 79; arrives, 82; becomes an A. M., 91; obligation of Brown University to, 96; resigns, 103; an evangelist, 104; removes to Newark, 109; death of, 151.
Emigrant church, 40.

Emporium of Baptist influence, 183.
Episcopalians, reply to, 35, 38; worship in Keithian house, 64, 65.

F

Fasting and prayer, 117, 118.
Feeble churches fostered, 74.
First Baptist Church, constituted, 31; in danger of losing property, 64; distinctly organized, 69; constituent members, 70; Communion Service of, 79; new meeting-house of, 86; unincorporated, 142; moves for a missionary society, 156.
First Baptist meeting-house built, 63.
First Baptist Sunday-school, 186-188.
Fleischman, Konrad A., 195.
Fleeson, Thomas, at Roxborough, 155.
Ford, Phillip, 18.
Frankford Church, constituted, 169; pioneer laborers of, 170; pastors of, 190.
Funerals in military or Masonic order, 176.

G

Gano, John, in Philadelphia, 80; called to First Church, 125, 127.
Gilbert Curtis, 147.
Gill, John, D. D., 82.
Government, frame of, 17.
Graveyard, Fifth street, 50.
Griffith, Benjamin, arrives, 47; ordained, 58; collects records of churches, 72; death of, 96.
Grigg, Jacob, 189.

H

Hart, Oliver, 71.
Harvard College, donations to, 56.
Holcombe, Henry, 180.
Holy Spirit poured out, 158.
Hollis, Thomas, donations of, 56.
Holme, John, purchases land, 18; a magistrate, 27; prominent, 31.
Holme, J. Stanford, 18.
Holmesburgh Church, 18.

Honeywell, John, will of, 138; school fund, 138.
Hopewell Academy, 76, 80.
Hymn Book, Baptist, 142.

I

Ide, George B., 195.
Independence Hall, 119.
Indian Deed, 22.

J

Jayne, David, 192.
Jenkins, Nathaniel, 73.
Jewel, Wilson, 195.
Jones, David, 128.
Jones, David, Jr., 180.
Jones, Horatio Gates, 165.
Jones, Horatio Gates, Jr., quotations from, 30, 40, 46, 68.
Jones, Jenkins, arrives, 47; at Pennypack, 59; in Philadelphia, 69; death of, 78; legacy of, 78.
Jones, Samuel, ordained, 43; death of, 55.
Jones, Samuel, D. D., portrait of, *frontispiece;* book dedicated to, 39; arrives, 65; in Philadelphia, 87; graduates, 88; license of, 89; ordination of, 89; settled at Pennypack, 90; instructs in theology, 107; first President of Trustees, 154; a noble repretative, 164, death of, 184.

K

Keach, Benjamin, 22.
Keach, Elias, arrives, 22; imposition of, 23; baptism and ordination of, 23; chief apostle, 25; resigns, 25; returns to England, 29.
Keen, Joseph, 150, 187.
Keith, George, 27.
Keithians, 27,28; articles of faith of 27; friendly to Baptists, 42; meetinghouse of, 43.
Keithian Quakers, 29.
Kennard, Joseph H., 194.
Killingsworth, Thomas, 28; death of, 46.

King, John, 182.
Kinnersley, William, assistant minister, 59; death of, 65.
Kinnersley, Ebenezer, 65; ordained; 68; opposed to Whitefield, 68; a scientist, 68; Professor of Rhetoric, 75; resigns, 106; death of, 106; memorial window to, 107.
Knollys, Hanserd, 31.

L

Latter Day Luminary, 191.
Laying on of hands, 25, 40, 41, 60, 139, 175.
Lee, Franklin, 195.
Letters of dismission, 59, 60; and recommendation, 151.
Letters of notification, 150.
Letters, blanks of, 166; the first from churches, 58.
Levering, Abraham, 72.
Levering, William, 72.
Levering, John, baptized.
Linnard, James M., 195.
London, sent to for a minister, 78; letter from Association to, 84.
Lord's day. observance of, 57.
Lord's Supper, and scattered members, 140; preceded by baptism, 139.
Lower Dublin Church, constituted, 23, 24; first meeting-house at, 44; new meeting-house at, 101; present meeting-house, 163; patriotism of, 120; trouble concerning property of, 72.

M

Malcom, Howard, birth of, 155.
Manning, James, in Philadelphia, 110, 121-124; called to First Church, 135; interest in Philadelphia Association, 140; first Baptist Doctor of Divinity, 140; death of, 148, 149.
Marriages, by dissenting ministers, 79; between believers and unbelievers, 57; legal, 168.
Mathias, Joseph, 53.

McLaughlin, James, 189.
Membership essential to official standing, 57.
Menno, Simon, a Baptist, 29.
Mennonites settle in Germantown, 29.
Messengers, names of first given, 61.
Minutes, wanting, 49; of Association first printed, 97.
Missionary Society, First Church moves for a, 156.
Missions Foreign, growing interest in, 157; collection for, 166, 177, 181, 184; Christian, 167.
Missionaries, sail for India, 183.
Moderator, name first given, 73; a member of an associated church, 160.
Montgomery County, when formed, 51, 140.
Montgomery Church, organization of, 51; services at, 52; meeting-house of, 52.
Morgan, Evan, ordained, 43; death of, 47.
Morgan, Abel, arrives, 48; settled at Pennypack, 48; Concordance and Confession of faith by, 55; death of, 55.
Murphy, J. R., quotation from, 24.
Murphy, J. C., at Frankford, 189.

N

New Britain Church organized, 75.
New Market Street Church, constituted, 190; build a meeting-house, 191.
Noble, Abel, the First Seventh-day Baptist, 39.
Northern Liberties, Church organized, 98; received into the Association, 104; a lot in, 155.

O

Ordination, certificate of, 76.
Ordination of deacons, 91.
Organ. sound of in Baptist worship, 86.
Orphan Society, 182.
Oxford Church property, 40.

P

Painful division, 48.
Parsonage, free, 176.
Patriotism of Lower Dublin Church, 120.
Peckworth, John P., 189.
Penn, William, 17, 19, 20; death of, 54.
Penn, Admiral, a Baptist, 19.
Pennypack, arrival of the first Baptists at, 21; meaning of word, 22.
Persecutions in Wales, 20, 21; in New England, 98-101, 107.
Philadelphia founded, 17.
Philadelphia Association, organized, 44; meets with closed doors, 58; chartered, 154; centennial of, 170.
Piscataway Church, 25.
Pitman, John, 120.
Preachers, supply of, 43.
Precentor, singing led by, 162.
Prerogative of the ministry, 181.
Presbyterians, and Baptists together, 32; separate, 34.
Presbyterians, letter to, 33.
Princeton student, 181.
Property, danger of losing, 64, 65, 72.

Q

Quakers, division among, 27.

R

Records, failure to keep Association, 66; First Church meagre, 78; of Association commenced, 72.
Religious liberty, in Philadelphia, 17; and the Baptists, 27, 64.
Revolution, conclusion of, 134.
Rogers, William, ordained, 105; chaplain, 120; Professor of Rhetoric, 143.
Roxborough, first preaching at, 72; first settlers, 144; Church constituted, 144; old meeting-house at, 145; constituent members, 146.
Ruling Elders, 50, 94.
Rutter, John, pastor at Blockley, 162; excluded, 167.
Rush, Dr. Benjamin, 20.

INDEX. 203

S

Second Baptist Church, in Church alley, 153.
Second Church, constituted, 158-160; worship in a lodge room, 160; meeting-house dedicated, 161; incorporated, 173.
Selby, Thomas, a disturber, 48; excluded, 49.
Seventh-day Baptists, 39, 50, 51.
Sisters permitted to vote, 93.
Slavery, abolition of, 146.
Sparks, Richard, bequest of, 50.
Stage to New York, 142.
Statistics of churches first given, 85.
Staughton, William, settles in Philadelphia, 164; prosperous, 165; indefatigable, 165; theological school of, 192.
Stillman, Samuel, born, 65; preaches in Philadelphia, 81; called to First Church, 103.
Sunrise, Association met at, 134.

T

Temperance, 142.
Theatres, 150.
Third Church constituted, 175.
Thomas, William, 53.
Tunes authorized to be sung, 143.
Tullytown Christian Church, 23.

U

Union M. E. Church, 90.
Ustick, Thomas, 135-137; death of, 161.

V

Vanhorn, P. P., ordained, 71; preaches at Roxborough, 72; resigns, 86.
Vaus, Samuel, an impostor, 21, 22.

W

Wales, and Pennsylvania Baptists, 18; persecutions in, 20, 21; Baptist Association in, 21.
Walter, Joseph S., 158.
Warren Association, organized, 94; letter to, 95.
Washington, George, death of, 154.
Watts, John, pastor at Lower Dublin, 26; an author, 29; preaches in Philadelphia, 32; death of, 42.
Watts, Stephen, 91.
Weed, Dr. G., anxious to preach, 83.
Welsh Tract Church, 40.
Whitefield, George, arrives, 65; visits Jenkin Jones, 66; his church, 90.
White, William, ordained, 152; in Philadelphia, 162.
Williams, Roger, 18, 19.
Winchester, Elhanan, 128; apostacy of, 130-133, 135.
Windows, boards in, 125.
Wood, Joseph, ordained, 46; death of, 72.
Worship, orderly, 57.

Y

Yellow fever, 152, 153.

www.ingramcontent.com/pod-product-compliance
Lightning Source LLC
Chambersburg PA
CBHW020930230426

43666CB00008B/1620